CENTERED ON CHRIST

an introduction to monastic profession

CENTERED

ON

CHRIST

augustine roberts

Nihil obstat:

Rev. Basil Pennington, OCSO
Censor Deputatus

Imprimatur:

+ BERNARD J. FLANAGAN
Bishop of Worcester

May 25, 1977

The Nihil obstat and Imprimatur are official declarations that a book or pamphlet is free of doctrinal and moral error. No implication is contained therein that those who have granted the Nihil obstat and Imprimatur agree with the content, opinions or statements expressed.

1505

LIBRARY OF CONGRESS CATALOGING IN PUBLICATION DATA

Roberts, Augustine, 1932-
    Centered on Christ.

    Includes bibliographies and index.
1. Monastic and religious life.   I. Title.
BX2435.R534   248'.894   79-4036
ISBN 0-932506-04-6
ISBN 0-932506-03-6 pbk.

248.8
R643c

Published by:

St. Bede's Publications / Box 61 / Still River, MA 01467

TABLE OF CONTENTS

PREFACE

In many ways, Christian monasticism seems called to be a special meeting place for the different religious currents which ebb and flow in the world of our times, a meeting place and a fountain of new life. This is particularly true of Benedictine and Cistercian communities which represent the mainstream of western monastic life. For this reason, monastic profession in these communities assumes a special importance and an adequate preparation for it must be made.

The present volume is meant as a help in entering into the meaning of such an act, both for the person who embraces the monastic life as well as for the community receiving the new nun or monk. Because of this specific purpose, a brief word about the book's genesis, structure, and use may be helpful.

The point of departure was a mimeographed booklet by Father Louis Merton on the monastic vows, distributed from Gethsemani Abbey in the early 1960s. As novice master, I made ample use of this work and wished to translate some of its best pages into Spanish for the sake of our monks in formation here at Azul, Argentina. It was during the years of the Second Vatican Council. As time progressed, it became increasingly clear that the developments in moral theology, in the theology of the Church, and in studies on religious and monastic life would demand considerable rewriting of Father Louis' material. This is what I have tried to do.

Many people have helped me. My gratitude is due, in the first place, to my beloved community of Azul, where the first version of the text was written and mimeographed in 1967. The Benedictine nuns of Santa Escolastica Abbey, near Buenos Aires, helped greatly in toning down the exclusively "Cistercian" character of the text and making it suitable for wider use in their revised edition of 1970. The first English version in 1975 would not have been possible without the initiative and generosity of the monks of Spencer, nor would this present revised and definitive edition have been achieved without the assistance of the Benedictine Oblates of Still River, Massachusetts. Many other people, especially the translators into other foreign languages, have helped in this revision by their criticisms and encouragement. To each of them, my sincere thanks. An abridgment of Chapter Six, which is the chapter most directly dependent on Merton's original notes, appeared as an article in *Cistercian Studies* in 1972. A detailed technical version of Chapter Seven was published in the same magazine in 1975.

The selected bibliography after each chapter contains those books, or sections of books, which were useful in writing the present work. It also includes those books published from 1965 to 1977 which have been recommended by Cistercian novice masters as helpful in formation.

The body of this work is made up of Chapters Two through Six, which deal one by one with the promises of profession. In each of these five chapters the analysis of the vow starts off with a clarification of the more exterior aspects and obligations, includes a word about possible infidelities in its regard, and ends with some remarks on its interior and more purely spiritual dimension. The book as a whole follows this same rhythm.

Chapter Seven takes up again the theme of *conversatio*, analyzed in Chapter Two, and attempts to present a unified and more systematic view of the many elements described in the preceding chapters. The final chapter develops at greater length the need, already expressed in the first chapter, of a lived experience and personal synthesis on the part of each monk or nun called to this way of following the Lord.

Thus this guide to monastic profession is meant above all for monks and nuns in formation. The approach is inspired by that of Thomas Merton, but many other lines of thought have been introduced in an effort to obtain a more compact and coherent synthesis. Since I lack Merton's gift of expression, the style is less flowing, but the general presentation of a popularized introduction to the life of the vows, rather than a technical study with footnotes and detailed references, has been maintained.

In this spirit I have simplified or side-stepped several disputed questions such as the *Rule of the Master*, the nature of authority in religious life, permanent commitments in general, and several more strictly historical points. Recent writings on these questions, however, have been taken into account. On the other hand, elements directly connected with the monastic vows, such as conversion of life, stability, and spiritual methods, receive extended treatments, since they are seldom dealt with in other books.

The premise which underlies this entire volume is that the monk's life can only be understood by seeing it as a union of two different spiritual movements present throughout the history of mankind and particularly significant in the world of today: man's desire for community and his search for personal union with the Eternal. The fusion, rather than the opposition, of these two deep currents of the spirit makes Benedictine life, at one and the same time, strongly *cenobitic* and clearly *contemplative*.

Different emphases here are possible, and even desirable. If the following pages tend to underline the contemplative element, it is due to the fact that the latter is more specifically characteristic of monastic life and orients the communal dimension. In this context the phrase, "contemplative life," should be taken in its modern western sense: a way of life totally ordered to the fullness of Christian prayer. Such a way of life does not exclude, but rather guarantees the real apostolic fruit of both community and contemplation. It does, however, put such fruit in second place. I do not attempt to justify this contemplative orientation, but rather take it as the key for interpreting the other elements of Benedictine-Cistercian life. Your use of these pages will depend to a large extent on your own personal approach to such an orientation.

In this sense, the growing interest in mysticism and methods of contemplation may mean that others besides Benedictines or Cistercians will be using this book. If so, it will simply be another sign of the "monk" hidden in every human heart. It should be easy for such readers to adapt the work to their particular needs and circumstances. Thus the chapters on chastity, poverty, and obedience are able to be applied without difficulty to other forms of Christian and religious life. The monastic experience of these evangelical counsels can be of help to all sincere Christians in appreciating more fully the Gospel's contemplative dimension.

The chapters on conversion of life, stability, and spiritual methods, though more specifically monastic, may actually be of greater general interest, since they point to the self-transcendence and inner integration which is at the heart of every truly human life. Here also, the concrete details should be adapted to one's personal vocation. The emphasis on a unified approach to the vows, which is contained in the monk's promise of conversion, can be especially helpful to other forms of Christian spirituality which sometimes tend to magnify this or that aspect of the Gospel out of proportion to the whole.

Along with examples from the Desert Fathers and from monastic tradition in general, you will notice an abundant use of the documents of the Second Vatican Council. This does not spring from a mere desire for illustrative texts, since many other such texts are available, nor from a rather human wish to quote an authority. It is rather because the documents of the Council, as extraordinary expressions of the Church's universal teaching office, speak directly to the light in us of the crucified and risen Christ which we call "faith." My conviction is that monastic life, more than any other form of Christian existence, must be continually built upon such faith. It alone can show us God's Word, purify our hearts, form us adequately for community and contemplation, integrate our own spiritual experience and tradition into the life of the Church, and lead us along the often obscure path through Christian hope to perfect love. This work of faith is the whole purpose of religious and monastic profession.

May these pages, then, in which such "new things and old" are closely interwoven, help to reveal more clearly the riches of the kingdom of heaven to those who seek God today. "And all this the Lord will manifest by the Holy Spirit in His workman now purified from vice and sin" (RB 7, 70).

A.R.

CENTERED ON CHRIST

To
Mary,
Mother of the Church

ABBREVIATIONS

AG   *Ad Gentes*. Decree of Vatican Council II on the Missionary Activity of the Church.

Conf. *Conferences* of John Cassian. English translation in Cistercian Studies Series (Kalamazoo, Michigan).

DV   *Dei Verbum*. Dogmatic Constitution of Vatican Council II on Divine Revelation.

GS   *Gaudium et Spes*. Pastoral Constitution of Vatican II on the Church in the World of Our Times.

LG   *Lumen Gentium*. Dogmatic Constitution of Vatican II on the Church.

PC   *Perfectae Caritatis*. Decree of Vatican Council II on the Appropriate Renewal of the Religious Life.

PH   *Persona Humana*. Declaration of the Sacred Congregation for the Doctrine of the Faith, on Certain Questions of Sexual Ethics (December 29, 1975).

RB   *Rule of Saint Benedict*.

SC   *Sacrosanctum Concilium*. Constitution of Vatican Council II on the Sacred Liturgy.

ST   *Summa Theologiae* of Saint Thomas Aquinas.

VS   *Venite Seorsum*. Instruction of the Sacred Congregation of Religious, on the Contemplative Life and the Enclosure of Nuns (August 15, 1969).

CHAPTER ONE

THE MEANING OF
MONASTIC PROFESSION

1. TWO ELEMENTS

The entrance of the postulant into the community is in itself a public commitment to follow Christ by the practice of the evangelical counsels. As such, the simple act of entry is a true experience of Christ who loves and invites the young monk, and who inspires at the same time his positive response. The vows pronounced later make this commitment more explicit and intensify the personal encounter with the Savior.

The most ancient rite of profession, dating from the beginning of Christian monasticism, was a good expression of this deeply personal and spiritual element. It consisted in a *change of clothing*. The candidate removed his former clothes and put on the rough tunic commonly worn by monks. A belt signified chastity and mortification. A hooded cape symbolized the humility of his new state. A scapular served for manual labor. In cenobitic monasteries, such as those of Saint Pachomius, the abbot would give the habit to the new postulant after a certain period of trial. By this change of attire the young monk publicly proclaimed his intention to renounce the world and his past life in order to give himself completely to the search for God in solitude and obedience. The habit was a permanent symbol of his conversion of life and of his new membership in the army of Christ.

With the passage of time there was added an *oral promise* of fidelity. Finally, in the sixth century, besides the change of clothing and the oral promise, Saint Benedict prescribed a *written document*, signed by the newly professed and placed by him on the altar during the ceremony of profession. This would serve as a witness of his profession and testify against him if in the future he were unfaithful to his promise (RB 58).

In these prescriptions we can see a juridic element being introduced into monastic profession, the purpose of which was to guarantee the primary element of total conversion. Nevertheless, the oral promise and written document show a gradual institutionalization of the Christian's response to the monastic calling. In the course of centuries this institutionalization increased and the act of profession assumed more and more the legal aspect of a contract between monk and community. Profession became the means by which the Church assures the monk's fidelity to the new life he has freely chosen under the inspiration of grace.

At the same time, scholastic theology and the new forms of religious life which arose in the Middle Ages obscured the more spiritual and monastic meaning of profession. Medieval thought attempted to synthesize and sum up the totality of the religious life in a few concrete and basic obligations: poverty, chastity, and obedience. These would be the essential renunciations of all forms of religious life.

Obviously we cannot reject or eliminate the juridical aspect of religious or monastic life, but we must relate it to the more primitive and purely charismatic element, seeing the intimate connection which exists between the two components. The juridical aspect, by stressing the minimal obligations of the vows, establishes the monk in a fixed state of life. It indicates the *matter* of his self-gift, the object of his commitment, that which he is sacrificing. The more interior and spiritual element, on the other hand, represents the *spirit* of the sacrifice. It gives meaning to the juridical obligations, is the soul of the life of the vows and the whole purpose of religious profession. The union of these two elements of his profession puts the monk in the heart of the mystery of the Church as described by the Second Vatican Council:

> The society furnished with hierarchical agencies and the Mystical Body of Christ are not to be considered as two realities, nor are the visible assembly and the spiritual community, nor the earthly Church and the Church enriched with heavenly things. Rather they form one interlocked reality which is comprised of a divine and a human element.... The communal structure of the Church serves Christ's Spirit, who vivifies it by way of building up the body of Christ (LG 8).

Many people, and even many religious, tend to think that the vows embrace only the minimal juridical obligations: "not to sin against chastity, not to have anything without permission, not to indulge self-will." But these are no more than points of departure for something much greater—the adventure of living completely *centered on Christ, in body, soul, and spirit*. The obligations of the vows are not imposed from without, like laws which restrict the liberty of spiritual growth, but blossom forth spontaneously from the heart of the monastic-contemplative life. They are simply the *duties of a special state of life* like those, for example, of a truck driver, of a doctor, or of an astronaut. A trucker cannot get drunk or fall asleep while driving in the night. These are intrinsic obligations of his state. Likewise, the keeping of the vows of his profession is an intrinsic obligation of being a monk. Not because Canon Law or the Rule imposes them, but because the monk has freely chosen a state of life in which all is oriented to the love of Christ.

Therefore, the first responsibility of the monk is to love with all his heart. The vows presuppose this love and express it exteriorly by incorporating us into a state of life which has no other reason for existence than the love of Christ. The *monk is a lover*, not only interiorly and spiritually, but also exteriorly and juridically. *And the monastic vows embrace the two aspects of this life of love.* They are distinguished one from the other in their juridical aspects, but they form one inseparable unity as instruments and expressions of the love of God calling the monk to a life of contemplative charity in the obedience of Christ. Profession is the door to this life.

2. THE VOWS ACCORDING TO SAINT BENEDICT

The shift from a simple, symbolic taking of the habit to a written, juridical promise took place gradually. In describing the ceremony of profession, Saint Benedict does not give us the actual formula which the novice read. The three points—stability, conversion of life, and obedience—appear to be named not so much as distinct vows but as three important aspects of the new life, which the novice is now well aware of from his reading of the Rule and his period of preparation (RB 58, 17-18).

Nevertheless, since the time of Saint Benedict, the words "stability, conversion of life, and obedience" have been adopted as very apt terms to designate the responsibilities assumed by the monk on the day of his profession. They appear in the formula of profession from the ninth century on. Moreover, the custom outside monasticism of considering the vows of poverty, chastity, and obedience as essential to the religious life makes necessary an explanation of the special content of our formula in which the words "poverty" or "chastity" are not even mentioned. In practice, an understanding of the three monastic realities referred to by Saint Benedict and promised at the time of profession is a necessary preparation for entering into the dynamism of monastic life. It is the purpose of this book.

The traditional formula of profession, used during the last eight centuries, says:

I, Brother N_____, layman (or priest, etc.), promise stability, conversion of life, and obedience according to the Rule of Saint Benedict, Abbot, before God and His Saints, whose relics are venerated in this place called _____ in the presence of the Reverend Father N_____, etc....

One notes first that the formula is not abstract, but concrete. "I promise stability...in this place." I promise to live and die in this monastery (if obedience does not send me to another place). I promise to change my life, to leave off living as a worldling and to live as a monk. I promise to obey the superiors in this house.

The saints are invoked as witnesses. This is done not only in general terms, but with concrete reference to the saints whose relics we have here, and especially to Our Lady, to whom the monastery is usually dedicated. Thus we see the public aspect of the vows: all heaven and earth now know that we have accepted God's call. And also the concrete aspect of our gift of self: God has chosen and I accept *this* monastery, with *this* form of life, *these* brothers, *these* superiors, *this* climate, etc. In the very act of profession the monk anticipates one of the paradoxes which is going to mark all his life of faith. The greatness and beauty of God is found in the most humble persons and things.

These vows do not so much imply a series of particular obligations as they do a total dedication of one's whole life. Thus the central core or axis of monastic profession will be the vow of "conversion of life" which embraces the basic methods by which the monk expresses his search for God. Because of its importance we shall treat it at once, before the other elements of his self-gift.

For Further Reflection

1. Is there a proper relation in your own life between the two primary elements of religious profession? Is Jesus a real person for you?

2. What are the principal evangelical counsels according to LG 42? When and how did poverty, chastity, and obedience overshadow the other commitments of profession?

3. In what sense is religious profession a "consecration" (LG 44 and PC 1)? Who consecrates, for what purpose, and by what means?

Bibliography

(The abbreviation, CS, indicates the *Cistercian Studies Series*, Spencer-Kalamazoo: Cistercian Publications.)

Cassian, J. *Institutes of the Cenobia*, Books I and IV. The Nicene and Post-Nicene Fathers of the Christian Church, 2nd Series, Vol. XI. Grand Rapids: Eerdmans, 1955, pp. 201-204 and 219-220. (To be published in a new translation by B. Ward in the *Cistercian Studies Series*, Spencer-Kalamazoo: Cistercian Publications).

Peifer, C. *Monastic Spirituality*. New York: Sheed and Ward, 1966, pp. 135-183.

Rees, D., et al. *Consider Your Call: A Theology of Monastic Life Today*. London: SPCK, 1978, pp. 110-117.

Region of the Isles, *Symposium on the Vows*. Nunraw, mimeographed at Mt. Melleray, Ireland, 1976, pp. A1-D22, (studies on the history of monastic commitment).

Vandenbroucke, F. *Why Monks?* CS 17, 1972, pp. 93-185.

SEE ALSO THE STANDARD COMMENTARIES ON RB 58:

Delatte, P. *The Rule of St. Benedict*. London: Burns and Oates, 1950, pp. 367-405.
de Vogue, A. *La Regle de Saint Benoit*. Sources Chretiennes 181-186, Vol. VI. Paris: Cerf, 1971, pp. 1289-1354.
Steidle, B. *The Rule of St. Benedict*. Canon City, Colorado, 1967, pp. 241-259.
Van Zeller, H. *The Holy Rule*. New York: Sheed and Ward, 1958, pp. 356-383.

WORKS ON RELIGIOUS LIFE IN GENERAL ARE ALSO HELPFUL, SUCH AS THE FOLLOWING:

Carpentier, R. *Life in the City of God*. New York: Benzinger, 1959.
Doyle, S. C. *Covenant Renewal in the Religious Life*. Chicago: Franciscan Herald Press, 1975.
Hakenewerth, Q. *For the Sake of the Kingdom*. Collegeville, Minnesota: Liturgical Press, 1971.
O'Doherty, E. F. *Vocation, Formation, Consecration and Vows*. Staten Island: Alba House, 1971.
Orsy, L. M. *Open to the Spirit: Religious Life After Vatican II*. Cleveland: Corpus Books, 1968.
Rahner, K. *The Religious Life Today*. New York: Seabury, 1976.
Regamey, P. *L'Exigence de Dieu*. Paris: Cerf, 1969.
Tillard, J. M. R. *A Gospel Path: The Religious Life*. Brussels: Lumen Vitae, 1975.
Van Kaam, A. *The Vowed Life*. Denville, New Jersey: Dimension Books, 1968.

CHAPTER TWO

CONVERSION OF LIFE

In the textual history of the Rule of Saint Benedict there has been a certain play on words between *conversatio* (way of life) and *conversio* (conversion). The latter word is used in the *Rule of the Master*, upon which the RB is based, whereas *conversatio* is more prevalent in the RB. Until recently the phrase, *conversatio morum*, which Benedict uses to describe the content of the young monk's solemn promise (RB 58, 17), was understood as "conversion of manners" or "conversion of life" taken in its more personal and subjective aspect—one's moral conduct.

But a better appreciation of the general context in which Saint Benedict wrote his Rule indicates that the phrase should be taken in a more objective sense: "Conversatio morum" *is the way of life which corresponds to the monastic calling.* It is a dynamic in which both personal conversion and community observances play their part. Taken in this sense, the phrase "conversion of life" still seems to express the rich meaning of the vow better than other possible renderings.

What, then, does this vow mean? What are the obligations it implies for us? And how do we enter into its spirit?

When the monk pronounces this vow, he promises to "live monastically." He embraces the whole life of prayer and asceticism which is at the heart of the monastic vocation. The monk is a convert from the worldly way of life and he embraces a new life—the monastic life. This new manner of living, in its turn, will bring him to the interior conversion of heart which is the whole purpose of the external way of life. Thus the first conversion leads to a way of life which points toward and facilitates a deeper, more interior conversion which can carry the monk to the inner core of his being. We can thus begin to see how the vow of conversion of life, since it refers to the totality of the monastic vocation, is the foundation of the vows of *obedience* and *stability*, and includes in itself *poverty* and *chastity*. But what does this life mean?

1. WHAT IS MONASTIC LIFE?

The monastic life, immediate object of the vow of conversion of life, does not mean only the interior, spiritual life of each monk, but also, and more directly, the external life of monastic discipline. Better still, *it is the life of monastic discipline in its true spiritual dimension*: the observances of one's own monastery taken and used by the monk as a precious instrument to encounter God and to grow in the image of Christ. It is the life of *service* to which Saint Benedict refers when he says, "We must establish a school of the Lord's service" (RB Prol., 45). It is the imitation of Christ who came "to serve and to give his life in ransom for all men" (Mk. 10:45). It is the service described by the Second Vatican Council: "The main task of monks is to render to the Divine Majesty a service at once simple and noble, within the monastic confines" (PC 9).

In his article on "Conversatio morum" in the *Dictionnaire de Spiritualité*, Dom P. Schmitz stresses the ascetical aspect of this service:

> The monastic life for Saint Benedict and Cassian consists in a life of constant struggle against the habits of the world, the vices, the passions and everything that can draw us away from God, and a life of continual effort to acquire virtues. It is the active part of the spiritual life, that which Cassian calls the "active life" (cf. Conf. 14).

This description is excessively one-sided and we shall soon see that both Cassian and Saint Benedict include a contemplative dimension in their concept of monastic life. Nevertheless, we can say that conversion of life is, in the first place, the monastic life in its active aspect of struggle against vice and growth in virtue. It is the "spiritual combat" absolutely necessary to make a monk. It is to be a "soldier of Christ," to belong actively and dynamically to a community in which "nothing is preferred to the love of Christ" (RB 4, 21).

Desert Fathers

This spiritual combat is described in many sayings of the Desert Fathers when they reply to the question of a disciple, "What should I do to be saved?" For example:

> A certain brother came to Abba Poemen and said: What ought I to do Father? I am in great sadness. The elder said to him: Never despise anybody, never condemn anybody, never speak evil of anyone, and the Lord will give you peace.

> Abba Pambo questioned Abba Anthony saying: What ought I to do? And the elder replied: Have no confidence in your own virtuousness. Do not worry about a thing once it has been done. Control your tongue and your belly.

> An elder said: Here is the monk's life-work—obedience, meditation, not judging others, not reviling, not complaining. For it is written: You who love the Lord, hate evil. So this is the monk's life-work—not to walk in agreement with an unjust man, nor to look with his eyes upon evil, not to go about being curious, and neither to examine nor to listen to the business of others. Not to take anything with his hands, but rather to give to others.

Not to be proud in his heart, nor malign others in his thoughts. Not to fill his stomach, but in all things to behave with discretion. Behold, in all this you have the monk.

From such sayings of the Desert Fathers and from both Christian and non-Christian monastic tradition, what characterizes the life of a monk is a *dynamism of renunciation that leads to the experience of ultimate reality.* There is a complete conversion of life—external life style, moral life, affective life, intellectual life. For the Christian monk, the beginning and the end of this dynamism is the person of Jesus Christ.

John Cassian

Cassian, writing in the fifth century, sums up the experience of the Desert Fathers as he adapts their tradition somewhat to the European culture of his time and thus prepares much of the spiritual ground plan for Saint Benedict's work a century later. In Conf. 3, Cassian describes three aspects or stages of the monk's life of renunciation. These three dimensions of monastic conversion are present from the beginning, but are expressed progressively with variable intensities, as we shall see more fully later.

First, *the external renunciations:* solitude and stability, celibacy, poverty, manual labor, fasts, non-violence, recitation of the psalms.

Second, and above all, *the internal renunciations.* Here is the conversion of the heart and interior purity, the virtues and attitudes which correspond to the external observances: humility, gentleness, fraternal love and patience, obedience, discretion, interior discipline, etc. This is the true "active life"—*an asceticism oriented toward the acquisition of inner Christian virtues and of their Queen which is charity.* It is an asceticism of humility because God gives His grace to the humble.

When the love and humility of Christ have taken possession of the heart, there is still place for another important realm of self-denial.

Third, *the contemplative renunciations:* the secret annihilation of the imagination and of the soul itself in order that the contemplation of God and the mysteries of Christ may blossom forth from a connaturality with Him and with His kingdom in us, until this kingdom comes to complete fulfillment in heaven.

For Cassian, the renouncements of body and of heart are mutually necessary. There can be no achieving interior purity without an asceticism composed of concrete and precise acts, and no ascetical observance without the inner virtue which governs it. This interplay of observances and inner attitudes forms an environment where continual prayer springs naturally from purified hearts.

Prayer, then, and the contemplative dimension of monastic life in general are included in the vow of conversion. In fact they are vital to it. The monastic experience consists precisely in the journey of the monk from the first renunciations to the last. It is the passage from the self-love of fallen humanity to the complete victory of the love of Christ.

Rule of Saint Benedict

The concept of the monastic life as a dynamic movement centered on Christ through a life of conversion and renouncement dominates the entire Rule of Saint Benedict, especially the Prologue:

> Return by the labor of obedience to Him from whom you have departed by the sloth of disobedience...renouncing your own will...in order to fight for the true King, Christ the Lord.... Let us follow His paths, taking for guide the Gospel, in order that we may merit to see in His kingdom Him who has called us. If we desire to abide in the dwelling of His kingdom, we shall not arrive at it except by running with good works.... Therefore, our hearts and our bodies must be prepared to fight under holy obedience to His precepts... and as we progress in our monastic life (*conversatio*) and in faith, our hearts will be enlarged, and we shall run with unspeakable sweetness of love in the way of the commandments of God. Thus we shall share by patience in the sufferings of Christ and, likewise, deserve to accompany Him in His kingdom (vv. 2-3, 21-22, 40, 49-50).

The same approach is evident in RB 7:

> Let him hold fast to patience silently in his inner heart when he meets with difficulties and contradictions and any kind of injustice, enduring all without growing weary or running away. For the Scripture says, "He who perseveres to the end shall be saved"...and secure in the hope of a divine recompense, they continue joyfully and say: "But in all these tribulations we triumph through Him who loves us."... Having climbed all these degrees of humility, the monk will soon arrive at that love of God which, being perfect, excludes all fear. By it, all that which before he observed not without misgivings, he will begin to keep without any labor, as it were naturally and by habit. No longer for fear of hell, but for love of Christ and connaturally, for the delight of virtue. All this the Lord will manifest by the Holy Spirit in His workman now purified from vice and sin (vv. 35-36, 39, 67-70).

Also in the Epilogue:

> Whoever you may be who hasten on toward the heavenly homeland, practice with the aid of Christ this little rule of initiation that we have sketched, and then, finally, you will arrive with the protection of God at the loftier

heights of doctrine and virtue that we have described (73, 8-9).

For the third renouncement, see RB 7 and 20:

The monk judging himself guilty at all times because of his sins, should believe himself at the dread judgment, and say continually in his heart what the publican of the Gospel said with his eyes fixed on the ground: "Lord, I am a sinner and not worthy to lift up my eyes to heaven."... How much the more, then, are complete humility and pure devotion necessary in supplication of the Lord who is God of the universe! And let us be assured that it is not in saying a great deal that we shall be heard, but in purity of heart and in tears of compunction (7, 64-66; 20, 2-3).

To sum up, the vow of "conversion of life...according to the Rule of Saint Benedict" signifies the personal giving of oneself to the daily struggle to correct our own negligences and grow in Christian virtue. It means to tend constantly to the perfection of humility in the monastic life and to the full implantation of the kingdom of God in body and soul. It implies perseverance in this life unto the end, because love remains unsatisfied until it fully possesses the beloved.

Saint Bernard of Clairvaux

Saint Bernard, for his part, gives a beautiful summary of the matter of the vow of conversion as the first Cistercians saw it:

Our way of life is rejection by men. It is humility, voluntary poverty, obedience, peace, joy in the Holy Spirit. Our way of life is subjection to a teacher, to an abbot, to a rule, to discipline. Our way of life is to apply oneself to silence, to practice fasting, vigils, prayer, manual work, and above all to hold on to the more excellent way which is charity, advancing in all these observances from day to day and persevering in them until the last day (Letter 142).

This is conversion of life!

2. COMMITMENTS OF CONVERSION

When we embrace the monastic life, we take on the "spiritual combat" as the essential commitment of the monk. Can we explain in more detail just what this commitment implies?

In the first place, we promise to *tend toward the perfection of the love of Christ through self-renouncement*. The vow of conversion of life makes explicit the principal duty of every person dedicated to God, as pointed out by the Second Vatican Council:

All the faithful, of whatever state or manner of life, are called to the fullness of the Christian life and to the perfection of charity (LG 40).

Let religious be especially solicitous in that, through them, the Church really shows the face of Christ better each day to the faithful and to non-believers (LG 46).

This basic obligation to tend to perfection is repeatedly underlined in books that treat of the religious state. They can be read with profit in connection with our vow of conversion.

In particular, we promise *fidelity in the use of certain well-defined ascetical means:*

-poverty and chastity

-the basic observances of our Order

-the inner attitudes or virtues which are the soul, the spirit, and the only real fulfillment of the observances

The evangelical counsels of *poverty and chastity* are thus included in this vow. Some authors have said that evangelical poverty and consecrated chastity are included rather in the monk's vow of obedience, but this opinion is not so much in accord with the monastic tradition of the three renunciations as we have just seen it. Neither does it make evident the essentially positive element of these two counsels which, moreover, are historically prior to obedience as special vows.

Thus what is said in works which treat of the religious vows of poverty and chastity ought to be applied to our vow of conversion of life. In Chapters Three and Four we shall point out the more salient monastic features of these two evangelical counsels.

The *basic observances* of the Order, lived in the place where we made the vow, constitute the principal matter of conversion of life. This is important. The novice who is preparing to make this vow learns how the life lived in his own monastery constitutes a withdrawal from the world for the sake of union with God. After experiencing it for a while, he decides to embrace the life as it is lived in this community. By doing so, he promises to live the monastic life not in some *ideal* form (which never exists), but according to the concrete observance of a stable and fervent house which he has chosen.

In all monasteries there are deficiencies and imperfections. When we come face to face with these weaknesses, our vow of conversion of life does not ask us to reform the monastery or to criticize the faults that are there, but requires that we ourselves be good monks and contribute our efforts to maintain the fervor and observance of the house.

But a *superior*, for his part, is obliged by his vow of conversion and by his particular service to the community to watch over the observance and to maintain it at a high level, that is to say, at a level sufficiently elevated to assure that the brothers are really living lives of "conversion" in a spirit of faith.

Following our general plan of procedure, we shall study these basic monastic disciplines first, since they constitute the exterior obligations of the vow, before reflecting on the inner attitudes to which they lead and of which they are expressions.

3. BASIC OBSERVANCES

Among the observances and customs we practice in the monastery, some are essential and pertain directly to the matter of the vow of conversion of life. Others are accidental and changeable, for example, the ceremonies during the divine office, vocal prayers, clothing, haircuts, etc. And many others are not strictly monastic observances because they already oblige all Christians, for example, fraternal charity, mutual service, the sacraments, a minimum of prayer, respect for superiors.

We can say that the particular concrete means that are inseparable from the monastic state and, therefore, form the matter of the vow of conversion of life are five:

-withdrawal from society (enclosure and silence)
-life of prayer (lectio divina and liturgy)
-austerity of life (fasts, vigils, etc.)
-common life (for cenobites)
-monastic work (especially emphasized by Saint Benedict and the Cistercians)

In order to understand the obligations implied in these five means of loving God, it is necessary to repeat that the vow of conversion of life is neither just a general promise to "tend to perfection," nor a vow to observe customs and ceremonies. It is a commitment to embrace and to live in depth *those corporal and spiritual disciplines without which the life would not be truly monastic.*

These disciplines are the elements that Vatican II referred to as essential to the organized contemplative life:

The institutes that are integrally ordered to contemplation, so that their members, in solitude and silence, in assiduous prayer and fervent penance, are free for the exclusive search for God, maintain always an eminent place in the Mystical Body of Christ (PC 7).

The observances which in other places the Council has called "the essential elements of the monastic institution" (AG 18) and "those exercises proper to the contemplative life" (PC 7), are described here in detail:

-withdrawal from society ("in solitude and silence")
-life of prayer ("in assiduous prayer...free for the exclusive search for God")
-austerity of life ("fervent penance")

To these three characteristics of the monastic-contemplative life we add two more, common to other religious institutes, but especially singled out by the Benedictine-Cistercian tradition: common life and monastic work.

Who, then, imposes on us the obligation to keep these observances?

No one. This is very important. We freely choose the obligations on embracing the monastic state. Therefore, even during the novitiate these basic disciplines are obligatory as duties of our state of life. Remember what we have already seen on this point in Chapter One: by religious profession, the observances form the matter of a public promise made to God and thus they oblige by virtue of religion, as acts publicly consecrated to God.

But the deepest meaning of these observances goes far beyond the virtues of justice or religion. The Council expressed it in these words:

With the practice of the evangelical counsels the perfection of charity toward God and neighbor is encouraged in a singular way (LG 45).

Charity animates and rules even the practice of the evangelical counsels (PC 6).

For those who receive the charism of the monastic-contemplative life, these observances have a double function and, therefore, a double obligation: they are *instruments* or points of departure for attaining the purity of a love that is both fraternal and contemplative, and *signs* which give testimony to and protect this special intensity of love. In this light, as concrete expressions of an exclusive love of Christ and of all men in Him, we embrace and fulfill them.

Withdrawal from Society

Solitude and silence separate us from society. It is because of them that such withdrawal becomes essential to the contemplative state. Their importance results from two factors: one, *personal and psychological*, the other, *social and ecclesial*.

Psychologically, solitude and silence are necessary for a life of prayer. They make us sensitive to the voice of the Lover who speaks not in the strong wind, nor in the earthquake, but in a "tiny whispering sound" (I Kings 19:12). The Instruction "Venite Seorsum" emphasizes this personal element, quoting a letter of Saint Bruno, founder of the Carthusians:

> In silence and solitude resolute men are able to recollect themselves and, so to speak, to dwell within themselves as much as they please, cultivating the buds of virtue and feeding happily on the fruits of paradise. Here one strives to acquire that eye by whose limpid glance the bridegroom is wounded with love, and in whose purity alone may God be seen. Here one is occupied in busy leisure, and rests in quiet activity. Here, as a recompense for the fatigue suffered in strife, God grants His athletes the reward they have longed for, namely a peace unknown to the world and the joy of the Holy Spirit. This is the better part that Mary chose, that shall not be taken away from her (VS II).

Christ in the desert consecrated this life of solitude and silence. After Him, its richest fruit is the person himself who has embraced such a life. The crucible of the desert experience, with its dryness and lack of human support, becomes a mother's womb in which the monk is made anew, thanks to the spiritual stamina and interiority which it stimulates. Through this interiority, the monk's solitude becomes a special form of presence in the world, putting him in a *new relation* to the entire universe.

It is true that solitude and silence reduce the possibilities of expression, but they do this only in order to open up new avenues of life, as is seen in this saying of Saint Anthony of the Desert: "The monk living in the desert is saved from three battles: those with his eyes, his tongue, and his hearing. One battle remains—the combat of the heart."

In the detachment of solitude and silence, false friends disappear. The monk's heart comes to the surface with its inner divisions and unexplored regions. Little by little, inner harmony is restored with its necessary conditions and demands. The inner fruit of withdrawal from society is the peace which the world cannot give, the restoration of the image of God.

The other function of solitude and silence is *social and ecclesial*, as a witness to the eschatological orientation of the mystery of Christ which Jesus Himself tried to explain to His disciples: "I came from the Father and came into the world. Now I am leaving the world to go to the Father" (Jn. 16:28). Thus Pope Paul VI could say:

> However much the Church asks the laity to establish and spread the Christian life in the world, even more does she desire that the example of those who really renounce the world shine forth and that it be shown clearly that the Kingdom of Christ is not of this world (Magno Gaudio, May 23, 1964).

The Constitution on "The Church Today" confirms this function:

> The gifts of the Spirit are diverse. He calls some to give clear witness to the desire for a heavenly home and to keep that desire fresh among the human family. He summons others to the earthly service of men (GS 38).

The Instruction "Venite Seorsum" adds:

> The prayer of Christ is like an apex toward which converges the universal activity of the Church. In this way contemplative religious, bearing witness to the intimate life of the Church, are indispensable to the fullness of its presence (VS III).

NORMS OF ENCLOSURE

Saint Benedict affirms that "to wander outside is in no way useful for the souls of monks" (RB 66 and 67), and almost all monastic reform movements have insisted on the importance of a return to the spirituality of the desert. This desert solitude is made concrete for us in a geographic separation from cities and towns and in the norms of enclosure.

We are all responsible for the observance of our enclosure. Permissions to leave ought to be for true necessity. Our trips out, visits of relatives and friends, communication by letter or telephone are governed by the limits imposed by the contemplative life. It belongs to the superior to set forth more detailed norms concerning the observance of enclosure or silence in conformity with the general norms of our Order or Congregation.

Habitual negligence of enclosure or silence would go against the vow of conversion of life. In the case of a brother who has a more or less standing permission to leave the monastery or to speak, but frequently abuses his function in the community or the confidence of his superior by going out when it is not necessary, batting the breeze, habitually giving himself over to worldly diversions (movies, secular magazines, smoking, etc.), it would be an infidelity against his vow of conversion and perhaps a sin of scandal.

Some isolated acts would also be morally dangerous, such as sending a letter, calling by phone or leaving the enclosure against the known will of the superior. These would be not only against the vow of obedience but also contrary to conversion of life. A similar situation is involved in a deliberate conversation against the norms of silence merely to satisfy a personal desire for communication. Much, of course, depends on the motivation behind such acts.

Life of Prayer

This is the second essential exercise of the contemplative life and, under charity, is the end of all the other particular means of the monastic state. Its importance is seen in this paragraph from the Conciliar decree directed to all religious. With even more reason, then, it concerns us as monks:

> Drawing on the authentic sources of Christian spirituality, let the members of communities energetically cultivate the spirit of prayer and the practice of it. In the first place they should take the sacred Scriptures in hand each day by way of attaining "the excelling knowledge of Jesus Christ" through reading these divine writings and meditating on them. They should enact the sacred liturgy, especially the most holy mystery of the Eucharist, with hearts and voices attuned to the Church; here is a most copious source of nourishment for the spiritual life (PC 6).

At the same time, its difficulty appears in this witness from the desert:

> They asked Abba Agaton, "Father, what is the most difficult virtue in the monastic life?" He replied, "Excuse me, I believe that there is no work more difficult than to pray to God. As soon as a man begins to pray, the demons come to distract him, since they know that no other work puts such obstacles to their action as prayer does. Whatever other work you undertake, provided you persevere in it, will have its rest, but prayer demands a struggle unto the last breath."

The Council pinpoints three concrete elements or means to a life of prayer. They obviously assume a prime importance for our monastic profession, and we shall treat of them one by one:

-application to the reading of Scripture or *lectio divina* by silence, reflection, meditation
-*a Eucharistic life*: Mass, Communion, visits to the Blessed Sacrament, thanksgiving
-the liturgy of praise expressed in the *Divine Office*

The minimal obligation of the vow of conversion of life in these matters is fulfilled by following with fidelity the horarium of the community, inasmuch as possible.

Lectio Divina

The subject matter of *lectio divina* is the Word of God. This Word comes to the monk in a variety of ways, both personal and communal: in Sacred Scripture, through the teaching of the Church, in the Eucharist and the rest of the liturgy, through the abbot and the brothers, as well as through concrete historical events.

Lectio divina goes beyond and underneath merely human information, or books and articles which are purely technical, theological, or pastoral in nature. It does, however, make use of such studies when necessary. The difference between lectio and study lies more in the attitude of the monk than in the reading material itself.

In their encounter with the Word of God, the monastic Fathers developed a whole method of prayer based on sacred reading. This method is expressed in the formula *lectio, meditatio, oratio, contemplatio,* which means that from his reading, assimilated by the active reflection of his reason, imagination, and other faculties, the monk passes to a more direct, more personal and intimate conversation with God, with Jesus, Mary, or the Saints. This more personal prayer is the spontaneous expression of our feelings and desires. The human heart opens up to the Lord in thanksgiving, compunction, petitions, and adoration. Many other methods of prayer, such as the "Jesus prayer," are simply expressions or applications of this basic rhythm, as we shall see in more detail in a following chapter.

According to this underlying rhythm, contemplation is the generally brief and passing experience of the intimate presence of God as He unifies one's whole being, thoughts, and desires in Himself in a central point of the heart which remains unknown, yet experienced. In its light, Scripture and the themes of Salvation History take on new meaning. This is the "pure prayer" mentioned by Cassian (Conf. 9, 3) and Saint Benedict (RB 20, 4). See also DV 21 and 25. According to Cassian, this unifying experience leads to a more permanent and stable state of union in which "one's whole life, all the movements of one's heart, constitute from now on a single and uninterrupted prayer" (Conf. 9, 18 and 10, 7). Such contemplation represents a fullness of love, and we shall come across it again in treating the spirit of the vows.

Basic to these different forms of prayer is the need to love God, the desire to know Jesus Christ, to be with Him, to "see the face of the Lord," to commune with His reality by approaching Him as we really are. A person who embraces the religious life without a need for some kind of such intimacy with God in prayer is making a great mistake. This does not mean that every monastic vocation is necessarily a vocation to the highest degrees of contemplative prayer as described by spiritual writers, but the fact remains that we have come to the monastery to seek God, and the chief way in which we seek God is in prayer.

Since this is so, habitual and continued neglect of lectio divina constitutes an infidelity against the vow of conversion of life. Although there can be a question in such cases of a personal crisis in faith, the root cause may spring from a lack of love. In any case, disdain and contempt for all prayer and for all interior life, with a deliberate abandonment of all prayer life outside of some purely exterior formalities, can constitute a serious sin against the vow.

In practice, such contempt is rarely found in the monastery. Before arriving at such a point, the monk usually leaves his vocation. The deliberate abandonment of the spiritual life, with a full understanding of the implications of such an act, is unlikely in a monk of our times, although it might have been possible in the era of decadent monasteries. In some circumstances, for example in case of scruples or excessive mental strain, the abandonment of prayer and spiritual reading can be necessary and would not imply any contempt.

EUCHARISTIC LIFE

What a privilege and responsibility is ours in being able to participate actively at Mass every day! Let us think of how many Catholics are not able to do it for lack of time, indifference, or other reasons. We live our Eucharistic life in their name, for all the people of God, and for all men. For us, ourselves, it is the "most copious source" of all spiritual and monastic life, since it gives us the very Humanity of the risen Christ.

The Eucharistic mystery is, in a very special way, the sacrament of unity. Our common redemption in Christ is represented and truly effected by it. The Eucharist thus becomes the center of sacred liturgy and of the whole Christian life, especially in its community dimension.

This is very notably made manifest at the conventual Mass, which unites the members of the monastic family around the altar and sacramentally binds their hearts together in the Body of Christ, to the praise of the Father's glory. At the present time, thanks to growth in the Church's sacramental practice, the Mass is the center of the monk's day, even though the RB—like many other documents of ancient monasticism—seems to be unaware of its daily celebration.

The monk has a deep need to frequent the sacraments, to prepare himself for the encounter with Christ which takes place in them, and to prolong this encounter by his thanksgiving. It would be a mistake to pass several successive days without even assisting at Mass when there is no reason for our absence. Love calls us to draw close to the Beloved who comes to meet us and fulfill in us His work of unity.

DIVINE OFFICE

The *Liturgy of the Hours,* or Divine Office, is the special work of the monastery, inasmuch as it expresses socially and publicly the nature of our life—a community of praise, free for God alone.

But this is not to say that every monk always has the same obligation to this public praise. According to monastic tradition the responsibility for the Liturgy of the Hours falls directly on the community as a whole, and only secondarily on each individual monk. It is a question of personal attractions, aptitudes, and duties.

Personal Participation in the Liturgy of the Hours

The special work of a Benedictine or Cistercian monastery is the celebration of the Divine Office, not in the sense that the monastery exists *for* the Office, nor that each monk must assist at all the Hours, but in the sense that the Office is the *clearest communal manifestation* of shared contemplative life. In it one clearly sees a group of men or women who "give themselves to God alone" (PC 7). It is a work that has no other justification than the glory of God. Better than any other community activity, it provides the specific witness which our life gives to the Church and to the world.

Therefore all the members of the community, and particularly the superiors, have a serious obligation by their vow of conversion of life to provide for the *common recitation* of the Hours of the Divine Office. For the monk obliged to the common Office, habitual or continual absence from it without sufficient reason would go against the vow, that is to say, against one of his fundamental duties of state, since he has committed himself to a community of prayer.

On a more personal and individual level, every monk is called to the loving search for God through a life of prayer. This search in prayer is carried out through the whole monastic day, not just in liturgical worship, but also in lectio divina, work, and the general service of the brothers. The Office recited or sung in common is indeed an important means to achieve this life of prayer, but the Liturgy of the Hours, as well as the other elements of the monastic day, can follow *different rhythms* in the life of the different members of the community. Nevertheless, they should all contribute to the community's unity within a healthy flexibility.

Thus the participation of each monk in the liturgy, the lectio divina, and the service of the community will vary according to different personal vocations or local circumstances within the unity of the monastic vocation. The concrete rhythm of each monk's participation is subject to the decision of the abbot who will take into account the calling, attraction, and aptitude of the monk, along with the spirit and norms of the Order or Congregation.

In general, however, each individual member of a monastic community has the responsibility of praying the Hours of his community's public worship even when he himself is not physically present with his brothers. This *personal obligation* is evident in the very beginnings of cenobitic monasticism (Saint Pachomius), is emphasized by Saint Benedict (RB 50), and is reflected in the general Church norms for the Divine Office (SC 95). The primary purpose of such norms is to protect and foster the absent brother's life of prayer. Secondarily they show the Church's desire to express both bodily and spiritually, in the individual person of the monk or nun, the visible priesthood of Christ interceding for all men at the right hand of the Father (Heb. 7:25). Such are, in fact, the two main purposes of the common Office itself.

The liturgical reform carried out in recent years under the influence of the Second Vatican Council has put special emphasis on two aspects of the Liturgy of the Hours, whether it is prayed in common or in private:

-*The authenticity of the Hours.* The purpose of each particular Hour of the Divine Office is the sanctification of the corresponding part of the day or night. This, of course, does not deny the fact that Christ is already Lord of time and eternity by His resurrection and ascension. On the contrary, the Office presupposes His Lordship and expresses it concretely, applying it to the here and now, that is to say, to the Christian in his or her life situation. In this way chronological time (*chronos*) becomes Christological time (*kairos*), the hour of salvation. As a sign and instrument of this Lordship of Christ, the liturgical Hour should be prayed during the part of the day to which it corresponds.

-*The diversity of the Hours.* The dawn and dusk Hours (Lauds and Vespers) are at the key moments of the day and, therefore, should not be omitted without a serious reason. Vigils (Matins, or Office of Readings) has a special importance due to its more contemplative nature. The Little Hours also have a real role to play throughout the day, but they are less important.

We should keep these principles in mind in carrying out our responsibility for praying the Office. No matter what our personal rhythm of participation may be, we should have a solid appreciation for the Liturgy of the Hours. It is a treasure house of spirituality. To recite it, in or out of choir, is one of the monk's great privileges. The Office is taken up by the universal Church and blessed by her as her own prayer:

It is truly the voice of the bride addressing her bridegroom; it is the very prayer which Christ Himself, together with His body, addresses to the Father. Hence all who perform this service are not only fulfilling a duty of the Church, but also are sharing in the greatest honor accorded to Christ's spouse, for by offering these praises to God they are standing before God's throne in the name of the Church their Mother (SC 84-85).

All of us should recognize in the sung Office the voice of our community, she herself the spouse of Christ, expressing in the name of all of us our common longing for union with God and with the Lamb who sits on the throne. We should embrace the many minor inconveniences and bothers which prayer in common, especially sung prayer, can imply. Let our spirit be one of living faith in the presence of Christ and in the eternal worth of the prayer of our Mother, the Church.

Concluding, let us not forget that the Liturgy of the Hours is only one part of our commitment to a life of prayer. Yet it is here that community and person meet in an organized sharing of praise to our common Lord. Thus we need a great esteem for two realities which are at the heart of the monastic vocation:

-The vocation, aptitudes, and *personal graces* of each brother. This is the most vital element of all, since it is the direct work of the Holy Spirit who distributes His gifts as He wishes. This is what determines, in the last analysis, the way in which we carry out and bring to fruition our life of prayer.

-The community's *liturgy of praise*, sung or recited in common, as an expression of the communion in love and adoration of those who seek the face of the Spouse. We all have a responsibility, according to our aptitudes, to acquire a liturgical and biblical instruction, principally concerning the psalms, in order that "our mind be attuned to our voice" (RB 19, 7 and SC 90).

Austerity of Life

This is the third observance of the contemplative life enumerated by the Council in "Perfectae Caritatis." We ought always to place before our eyes the example of Jesus in order to enter into the true spirit and practice of our austerities. Penance is meant to be a *sharing in the sufferings of Christ:* in His fasting, His nights of prayer, His work, His fatigue and humiliations. By austerities our will is strengthened, the body is subjected to the soul and the moral virtues are rooted in our whole being. God uses our austerities in order that our human personality, wounded by concupiscence, be reestablished in the image of

Jesus and give itself to His service and contemplation with full interior liberty.

In a more particular way, *abstention from food* and *night prayer* for the sake of increased attention to God are significant parts of monastic asceticism. *Fasting* and *vigils*, each in its own way, hollow out a new dimension in the monk's heart, touching us in two of our most vital life rhythms: *eating*, with its series of needs and satisfactions, and *time*, with its succession of days and nights, light and darkness. By means of these austerities we can begin to break these cosmic rhythms in union with Christ and transcend them through faith and prayer, to which such austerities are ordered. Thus we can open ourselves in humility of body and soul to the world to come, where all needs will be satisfied and all darkness banished.

OUR OBLIGATIONS

Benedictine or even Cistercian life is no longer excessively austere, physically speaking, and persons of generally good health can follow the common rule. So much the more, then, should we be careful not to exempt ourselves from the fasts and common austerities, e.g., vigils, monastic work, routine chores, simplicity in meals and clothing. The vow of conversion of life demands reserve in requesting legitimate exemptions. The safest way is to accept the exemptions imposed or pre-scribed and not to seek them. Nevertheless, one should ask when there is true need, especially if a spiritual director has advised it.

The following would normally go against the vow of conversion:

-excessive eating, especially between meals.

-not observing the fast of the community or seldom getting up for Vigils, even with permission, if there is no reason or need for the eva-sion. The normal monk can eat less once in a while and rise early. He needs to do so to strengthen his response to grace and to avoid more serious weaknesses.

-likewise, an habitual seeking of pleasures, comforts, and permis-sions far beyond the norms of the community.

The Vatican Council (PC 7) used a very significant word in describing the austerities of the contemplative life—"alacer," that is, *fervent, joy-ful, enthusiastic*. It is the same teaching of Saint Benedict in citing the words of Saint Paul in his chapter on obedience: "God loves the cheerful giver" (RB 5, 16). What ought to distinguish the penance and austerity of the Christian monk is joy and enthusiasm.

We can fail against the spirit, and even against the letter, of the vow of conversion of life by a sadness or lukewarmness that destroys much of the value of our observances. Let us ask the Blessed Virgin, Mother of our Joy, to help us by showing us the cause of our lack of fervor and by giving us her own holy joy.

In practice, the obligations of austerity of life are fulfilled by accepting the ordinary penances with an enthusiasm born of faith. These penances are usually just the elements or disciplines that form an integral part of the Rule and the life of the community: the form of work by which we support ourselves, the horarium, the spiritual and atmospheric climate of the monastery, the diet, etc.

To live in the luxury of a rich person, without any corporal penance or active work, would be a betrayal of the vow of conversion of life.

Common Life

This fourth basic observance of monastic life is the primordial expression of the evangelical poverty which we promise. The common life was strongly stressed by monastic legislators prior to Saint Benedict, such as Saint Pachomius and Saint Basil (4th century) and Saint Augustine (5th century). It is a central element in the Benedictine-Cistercian tradition.

At the same time, it is a continual and eloquent testimony to the *presence of Jesus* in the midst of His people. Christ, risen and glorified, sends His Spirit to gather all men together in a community of faith, hope, and love. The unity of the brethren and the full sharing of goods among them will be the irrefutable sign of this new life and of their victory over selfishness and death: "Where two or three are gathered together in my name, I am in the midst of them" (Mt. 18:20). The common life constitutes, in the same way as consecrated virginity, a living and provocative sign of what the life of every Christian will be after the last coming of Christ.

The Council proclaims this in strong terms:

As the first-born of many brethren, and through the gift of His Spirit, the Word Incarnate founded, after His death and resurrection, a new brotherly community composed of all those who receive Him in faith and in love. This He did through His Body, which is the Church. There everyone, as members one of the other, would render mutual service according to the different gifts bestowed on each. This solidarity must be constantly increased until that day on which it will be brought to perfection. Then, saved by grace, men will offer flawless glory to God as a family beloved of God and of Christ their Brother (GS 32).

Seen in this light, a monastic community is not simply a more or less happy gathering of a group of nice people. It is the *concrete expression, here and now, of the great mystery of reconciliation and unity of all mankind under the headship of Christ*. This vision, based on faith, is especially important for communities whose members have very divergent personality traits. Our vow of "conversion of life...in this place" requires both this vision and our total dedication to its concrete expression here and now.

The Vatican Council itself, in its decree on the missionary activity of the Church, has stressed the importance of the common life for contemplative monasteries:

> These communities are urged to found houses in mission areas, as not a few of them have already done. Thus...they can bear splendid witness there among non-Christians to the majesty and love of God, as well as to man's brotherhood in Christ (AG 40).

It is significant that the "Declaration on Cistercian Life," by the Cistercians' General Chapter of 1969, cited this text. By his life in common, the monk fulfills an important *prophetic mission*, not only in behalf of the explicit members of the Church, but for all men.

What are our responsibilities in this matter? Common life includes:

-common liturgical prayer
-common work
-meals and food in common

The positive obligation of the common life is *regularity* and *punctuality*. This is very important, especially in the novitiate when the young monk forms habits which will influence the rest of his life. What God looks for from us is not mere exterior conformity, but the active love which expresses itself in uniting ourselves with the community as much as possible. It means witnessing to the *presence of Christ* in community exercises, fulfilling even the details of our obligations, and applying ourselves generously to the work at hand in order to support the community.

An habitual negligence in the common exercises, accompanied by disdain, pride, or laziness would go against the vow of conversion of life. For a grave sin something positively and seriously mundane would be necessary. We will see more details concerning the sharing of material goods when treating of monastic poverty. Common life is the *principal and indispensable expression of this poverty*.

The Rule itself indicates that the abbot can *dispense* a monk from some obligations of the common life when there is sufficient reason, i.e., health, age, work or another serious motive. Nevertheless, we should guard ourselves against abuses that can weaken the common life and the spirit of conversion.

A spirit which seeks *privileges, special permissions* and *escapes* is the greatest enemy of the common life. Love is not a leveler. It wants the necessary exceptions for others, but love does not demand ease and comfort *for itself.* We fail in this regard when we pile up (with or without permission) useless or superfluous things in a private corner. This seriously prejudices our prophetic mission of union in Christ. *Christ is our only good.* Only God can satisfy us. Our common life and our monastic poverty ought to proclaim this reality with deeds. At the same time, however, we must show the goodness of Christ not only with an empty desk or private box, but above all with the joy of a sincere love which is free of all inner obstacles.

A tendency to *avoid others* would also be against the common life. This includes fleeing from the presence of individuals or from the community in general, cultivating exclusive friendships, or not participating in community meetings without sufficient reason. Common life is the opposite of a rigid life, but what has to be avoided is an antisocial tendency.

Monastic Work

In the Christian tradition, work, fifth of the essential exercises included in our vow of conversion, has always been considered as a basic element of the monastic life. From the beginning, monks have taken to heart Saint Paul's admonition against certain "spiritual" Christians who refused to work under the pretext that the Parousia was imminent:

> We command you, brethren, in the name of our Lord Jesus Christ, that you keep yourselves free from every brother who leads an idle life, contrary to the teachings you have received from us.... Indeed, when we were still among you, we gave you this norm: "He who does not work, should not eat." Nevertheless, we have been informed that some among you live in idleness, without any other occupation than curiosity. Well then, such as these we exhort and admonish in the Lord Jesus Christ that, working orderly, they earn what they eat (II Thess. 3:6-12).

FUNCTION OF WORK IN THE LIFE OF THE MONK

Why this great concern about work for persons dedicated to a life of prayer and contemplation? Various reasons have been given, each with its share of truth:

-The monk *separates himself from the world*. Work is necessary so that he need not depend on the alms of seculars. The monk works to support himself, as Saint Paul told the first Christians. Thus the famous words of Saint Benedict: "Then are they truly monks when they live by the labor of their hands, like our Fathers and the Apostles" (RB 48, 8).

-The monk leads a *penitential life*. Work, with its sweat and fatigue, is the first and principal penance imposed by God on the human race (Gen. 3:17-19). This painful aspect of work is also foreseen by Saint Benedict: "If the conditions of the place or their poverty require that they occupy themselves in gathering in the harvest, let them not be saddened" (RB 48, 7).

-The monk is dedicated directly or indirectly to *Divine Worship*. Therefore, his work has a liturgical value and even a contemplative value by its relation to the liturgy. It sustains a community of praise and adoration. It constitutes the matter offered to God in the Mass, in a way analogous to that of the builders and artisans of the Tabernacle in the desert (Exod. 31) or of the Temple of Solomon (I Kings 6). In this sense every brother cooperates in the Divine Office by means of his work. Nonetheless, as an explanation of the meaning of monastic work, this exclusively liturgical approach does not sufficiently take into account the *personal and particular needs of the monks*. The true matter of the sacrifice of the Mass is not the work of the faithful, but *themselves*. It is true that our work is liturgical and that it is related to worship, but only insofar as it *passes through us*. The support of the community is always secondary to the true work of the community—to bring the monk through love to personal union with God in Christ.

-The monk is a *complete man*. He is an example for the laity in the world. Therefore, he ought to show by his life that work is a dignity for man, not only a difficulty, a penance, but rather an honor and a joy. Man shares in the creative action of God by means of his work according to God's commandment to Adam (Gen. 1:28), "Fill the earth and subdue it." Besides, man, when united to Christ, redeems the world by his work. He consecrates it to God and thus prepares the new world that will exist after the final resurrection. Saint Benedict refers to this dignity of work in the famous phrase that finalizes the chapter on the artisans of the monastery: "Let God be glorified in all things" (RB 57, 9).

Which of these different approaches is the best? How should we look at and fulfill our work?

The truth is that there is much value in each of these four approaches to monastic work, but none touches the heart of our vocation. For example, there is a true consecration of the material and human world by means of our work, but to base it on its value as a consecration or as an example to others would be like explaining a doctor's medical instruments by their value as reminders to others that physical fitness is a good thing. It's true that physical fitness is important, but the purpose of stethescopes and scalpels is to restore or defend physical health through the skill of the doctor, not just through the admiration of possible patients or onlookers. Similarly, work is an instrument in the hands of the monk to be used in his personal mission of restoring all things in Christ, renouncing the world's life-standards, and thus showing that the kingdom of Christ is not of this world.

Before all else, then, the monk is a *lover of Christ*. He is a skillful worker in His service, ready to fight the spiritual combat against the vices and spirits of evil which are within himself. He does not want to have any reason to exist apart from the Beloved. So he renounces everything, even the privilege of directly consecrating the world, in order to seek the face of Christ and encounter there the glory of the kingdom of God. This is the monastic life and the source from which its other elements flow.

Now in this search for the fullness of Christ's presence there is a danger to avoid and a goal to achieve. In both cases, manual labor plays an important role. First, the very real danger that lies in wait for the monk in his search for Christ is lukewarmness, laziness, idleness. Cassian calls it *acedia*: that lack of enthusiasm for the exercise of the spiritual life—prayer, reading, discipline, austerity—that all of us suffer from time to time. Human nature cannot read, pray, fast, or be still all day long. It needs to work in order not to degenerate through atrophy of the faculties.

In fact, work is perhaps the activity most typical of man. It is the field where the social and moral virtues that are indispensable for an authentic life of prayer grow and develop: patience, the sense of responsibility, prudence, self-discipline, perseverance, humility and renouncement of one's own judgment, cooperation and dialogue with others. Thus monastic work aims at the *transformation of the monk*, without denying the value of consecration of the world. Actually, man's transformation is the most central part of consecrating the world. Saint Benedict indicates this ascetic value of work at the beginning of his chapter on daily manual labor: "Idleness is the enemy of the soul. Therefore, at certain times the brothers should be occupied in manual labor" (RB 48, 1).

But the value of monastic work goes far beyond the prevention of acedia and touches the goal of life itself. *It is encounter with Christ,* above all by being an expression of evangelical poverty. This aspect of work was strongly underlined by the first Cistercians ("poor with the poor Christ"), as we shall see in more detail in treating of monastic poverty. For now it is enough to indicate that many of our obligations in regard to monastic labor flow from having embraced a state of *poverty* in imitation of Christ.

Experience also teaches that work is generally the element of our life in which we most exercise the vow and virtue of *obedience*. Let us look at it, then, as a special meeting place with the saving and transforming will of Christ. In this sense it is much more than a mere means of mental equilibrium. Jesus is there, active and dynamic, but also sorrowful and tired.

At the same time, we ought to recognize the other values of work, which are not of themselves opposed to its ascetical and Christological values, but rather contribute in a very positive manner to these values, insofar as they foster a life of faith. Thus there is hospitality, the support and service of the community, the necessary intellectual work, the beauty of the monastery, the development of human talents and personality, etc.

But it will always be necessary to return to the basic principle—work is an *ascetical exercise* at the service of the contemplative charity of each monk. Therefore, the primary norm that governs monastic work is not what will be achieved in an external way, but rather what it will do for the monk himself. The problems of economic support and of hospitality ought to be resolved from this fundamental need, and not vice versa. The personalistic and supernatural point of view must be affirmed—the work of the monk is not principally a means of production but a protection for the contemplative life and a real participation in Christ's redeeming humility.

Responsibilities Regarding Work

-Embrace the spirit and healthy traditions of *your own community,* Congregation or Order.

For example, the tradition of the Benedictine Order tends to stress intellectual work, whereas the Cistercians put more emphasis on manual labor. In both traditions there is a variety of nuances according to the local community, but they both regard their respective types of work as *services to the community* in behalf of the special charisms of the local house.

-Accept the conditions of the work imposed by obedience and by divine Providence.

The monk lives his conversion of life, poverty, and obedience by means of his fervent yet disinterested and submissive attitude toward the work of the monastery. He does not seek interesting work for himself, nor does he try to manipulate his surroundings in order to have agreeable tasks. At the same time, he accepts the betterment of the conditions of work insofar as it makes the work more productive and efficient for the maintenance of the house.

The monk is not his own boss. Therefore, he will have to content himself with conditions of work that are not ideal, such as inadequate tools or insufficient leadership. It is true that communal poverty implies that the work be well organized, but personal poverty makes us accept the lack of ideal conditions if there is nothing clearly indicated that we can do.

But the one in charge of a work project who loses time, misuses tools, or does the work badly by his own negligence, obviously offends against conversion of life.

-All that forms part of our work has been consecrated by our baptism and is elevated by our vow of conversion of life to an explicit expression of Christian poverty. So learn how to work and apply yourself to work with enthusiasm, patience, and perseverance. Perfect yourself as a worker in order to work with skill. Monastic labor demands more than mere good will. It requires intelligence and, at times, study.

-Don't request a dispensation from work for slight reasons. A common cold or headache is not sufficient reason to absent oneself from work. Be open with superiors in this matter, but also think of the many workers in the world who cannot dispense themselves from work for such things.

-Use your talents and time as the superiors wish, even when it might be arduous and demand sacrifices that seem beyond your strength. It is always legitimate, and many times advisable, to communicate to superiors our attractions, tastes, or personal weaknesses. The superiors should know the brothers well. But when there is this personal knowledge, you can presuppose that the superior knows what he is doing. Embrace the assigned task in a spirit of faith.

-Accept the humility of common work or of house chores that seldom are exciting and can often be boring. Cultivate a deep respect for

this type of work, which is a typically monastic occupation. Christ is especially present in it. It brings with it a very special grace, renders modest but indispensable services to the community, and is more protected by its humility from the dangers that beset other more specialized forms of work.

   -*Develop an attitude of courtesy, affability, and patience*, with special attention to the needs and comfort of those working with us.

4. INFIDELITIES AGAINST THE VOW

Apostasy and Flight

   By the vow of conversion, we promise to lead a converted life in the monastery. Thus the most direct infidelity against the vow would be to abandon the monastic state and the search for Christian perfection without a valid reason in order to return to secular society and the customs of the world. This is the most obvious case of a serious breach of the vow.

   The general norms of the Church refer to this abandonment of religious life as "apostasy" and "flight." Canon Law can be consulted on this point in case of need. When the act is consummated illegitimately and without permission, the apostate or fugitive is not free of the obligations which he assumed at the time of his religious profession. For his own peace of conscience and his personal integrity, he should return without delay to his community, or at least reestablish contact with the superiors. The latter, for their part, should show the qualities of the prodigal son's father (Lk. 15:20-22).

   The sin of apostasy or of flight can be purely *interior*—the formal and deliberate intention to flee from the monastery contrary to religious obedience. Even before being put into effect, such an option would be an offense against the vow of conversion.

Summary of the Negative Obligations

   To sum up the minimal obligations of the vow of conversion of life, we can indicate the following *serious infidelities*:

   -A serious violation of poverty or chastity.

   -Illegitimate abandonment of the monastic life, permanently by apostasy or temporarily by flight.

   -It can be a serious infidelity against the vow to leave the monastery without permission when one thus exposes himself to an occasion of grave sin or of giving scandal. There is also a question here of the vow of obedience.

-There is probably serious infidelity when the monk shows complete disdain for all the corporal observances and spiritual disciplines of his life, without in any way using the essential means of perfection which the monastery provides.

-It is possible that there be a serious sin against conversion of life when the monk refuses to use any remedy whatsoever against a moral vice, or when he does absolutely nothing to avoid the loss of his vocation. There is involved here an existential rejection of growth in the kingdom of God.

There are also *less serious infidelities* against the vow of conversion:

-Lack of regularity, a voluntary tepidity in the spiritual life, laziness at work, etc. Much depends on the degree of disdain for the basic observances of the monastic life.

-Habitual attachments to the pleasures and affairs of the world which are opposed to the monastic life. These are probably the most common infidelities, though they depend in great part on the person and on circumstances such as the culture of the country in which we live, age, or health.

Negligence or carelessness in the observance of less important monastic customs does not necessarily constitute a sin. It could be a voluntary or involuntary imperfection. Let us remember what we saw at the beginning of this chapter—the vow of conversion of life embraces only the *essential* observances, without which the life would not truly be monastic and, for us, Benedictine or Cistercian. The details of observance are opportunities to love rather than occasions to sin. In this spirit, in order to live the full meaning of conversion of life, to grow in the intensity of love of God, and to avoid greater faults, we should be regular and faithful even in these lesser responsibilities.

5. THE SPIRIT OF CONVERSION

We have seen the meaning of the vow of conversion of life: to live in accord with the grace of the monastic vocation, to embrace and use with fidelity the particular means that the monastic state offers for seeking God and for growing in the likeness of Christ. Then we saw in more detail the makeup of these basic observances of monastic asceticism, and we have just mentioned the acts and attitudes which would go against them and against the vow.

These infidelities simply indicate a *negative* aspect, the lack of a necessary minimum coherence between word and deed. Even the monastic observances do not constitute more than the *material* element of the vow, which is necessary but very incomplete in itself. Let us now look into the *spirit* of conversion of life, the soul and purpose of the observances, the outreaching force of the monastic way of life.

Principal Factor in the Monastic Life

Thanks to our vow of conversion of life, the main purpose, in fact the *only* purpose of our state of life is made explicit—to enter fully into the kingdom of Christ and to let His kingship enter into us. The other vows thus appear in their true light. They find their true meaning as particular applications of the vow of conversion of life:

-We rid ourselves of the spirit of the world by renouncing a worldly manner of life.

-We put on Christ by interiorizing a new manner of life.

Consecrated chastity, poverty, obedience, and stability are distinct ways of expressing this single spiritual thrust of renouncement and acquisition. We shall see this inner unity at greater length in Chapter Seven. It is important to realize also that conversion implies an interiorization not only of a life style, but of Christ Himself, who evidently is above and beyond any mere life style.

In particular, the vow of conversion of life includes and goes beyond obedience. We have already seen that it is possible to fail against conversion of life without failing against obedience, for example, by accumulating things in a private place with permission or by abusing a permission to leave the enclosure. On the other hand, one can be unfaithful to obedience without directly touching the minimal obligations of conversion, for example, by an isolated act of disobedience. Obviously this goes against the *spirit* of conversion. Nevertheless, we can see that a monk can be exteriorly faithful to obedience, yet lack a true monastic spirit.

So it is a mistake to treat of obedience as if it were everything in the life of the monk and all the rest subordinated to it. Obedience is indeed *an instrument and a sign* of conversion of life, its most powerful and necessary weapon, but the motivating force behind any act of obedience should be nothing less than the proclamation of the Lordship of Christ over the entire life of the monk. Chapter Five will provide a more extended treatment of this relation between obedience and conversion.

Spirit of Passover

We have already noted that many elements of monastic asceticism correspond to distinct aspects of the human life, passion, and resurrection of Christ. In fact *all* the monk's spiritual combat has a strong paschal and baptismal character.

> Hence to withdraw into the desert is for the Christian tantamount to associating himself more intimately with Christ's passion. It enables him, in a very special way, to share in the paschal mystery and in the passage of Our Lord from this world to the heavenly homeland. It was precisely on this account that monasteries were founded, situated as they are in the very heart of the mystery of Christ (VS I).

Monastic profession is often described as a second baptism but beyond the act of profession itself, all the life of the vows is marked with the sign of the paschal mystery, the passage of Christ to His Father. We receive this mark interiorly with baptism. By religious profession the monk "is more intimately consecrated to divine service in order to derive more abundant fruit from this baptismal grace" (LG 44).

The vow of conversion of life underlines this paschal spirit. "To fight for the true King, Christ the Lord" (RB Prol.) involves a continual passing from this world to the Father. It is a clearing of the way for the Spirit of the risen Christ. The monastic observances constitute, even externally, a dying with Christ to the works of the world and a rising with Him to a new life in His kingdom. *The spirit of the vow of conversion is simply to bring to fulfillment, in a monastic context, the promises of baptism* that we renew every year during the Paschal Vigil: "We renounce the Devil and his works, and we promise to serve the Lord faithfully in the holy Catholic Church."

As Mother Church, returning love for love, is on watch during the Passover night, remembering the death of Christ and celebrating His glorious resurrection, so also the monk promises to be always on watch, embracing with profound joy the renouncements of monastic observance in order to die to himself, to live in body and soul the life of the risen Christ, and thus to pass with Christ to the Father.

Leaving the World

In order to pass to the Father it is necessary to leave the world. We have seen that conversion of life includes withdrawal from society as a fundamental element. Now, this physical movement toward the fringe of society is no more than a means and a sign of a deeper and more enduring separation—"to make oneself a stranger to the conduct of the world," as Saint Benedict says (RB 4, 20).

What is this "conduct of the world"? Obviously it does not mean the professions and tasks of the world, such as those of a carpenter, factory worker, doctor, or student. Much less does it signify "the world of men" in its positive Christian reality as

> the whole human family along with the sum of those realities in the midst of which that family lives; the world which is the theater of man's history and carries the marks of his energies, his tragedies, and his triumphs; that world which the Christian sees as created and sustained by its Maker's love, fallen indeed into the bondage of sin, yet emancipated now by Christ, who was crucified and rose again to break the stranglehold of the Devil, so that this world might be fashioned anew according to God's design and reach its fulfillment (GS 2).

With this world, in fact, the monk becomes more and more deeply united by means of his special contemplative insertion into it!

The world from which the monk wishes to separate himself signifies rather a mode of activity which does not come from the kingdom of heaven. It is the search for a security in this world, the hunger for human praise, the selfish use of people, the desire to have more than is necessary, the manipulation of others for one's own advantage, the drive to seek success with the least possible effort, to avail oneself of deceit and privileges, fleeing from difficult situations, escaping responsibilities, seeking to dominate others, driving a good bargain, enjoying oneself. Such is the "wisdom of this world" (I Cor. 3:19) which can be active, as we know, within the monastic enclosure and within ourselves.

Now in this type of conduct, as Vatican II points out, the devil is often operative, and, therefore, the perspective of withdrawal from society is not at all a mere matter of behavioral norms, observances, or ethics. Neither is it a question of psychology, a philosophy of life, a back-to-nature movement, or contempt for the world. It is something deeply personal and *eschatological*: by his ascetic life on the margin of society, oriented toward contemplative charity, the monk is a witness of Christ who proclaims in action God's final victory over the "Prince of this world" (Jn. 12:31 and 16:11). He is a son and soldier of the Church in the death struggle against the spirit of evil. In and with the monk, the people of God can "pass from this world to the Father" (Jn. 13:1).

It is true that every baptized Christian must leave the world spiritually. The layman who consecrates the world by his activity in it does so without belonging to it. But God asks something more from a religious, and especially from a monk. He asks a *correspondence on the corporal level to that separation from the world which obliges everyone on the spiritual level.* It is this that explains the words of Paul VI which we have already quoted:

> However much the Church asks the laity to establish and to spread the Christian life in the world, even more does she desire that the examples of those who really renounce the world shine forth and that it be seen clearly that the Kingdom of Christ is not of this world.

In the world, the laity consecrate the fruit of the work of their hands. But by leaving the world the monk consecrates not only the fruit, but the whole tree down to the roots of his being. He shows that man has been created for a kingdom which is not of this world: "Christ died for all men, and there is only one final vocation for man, the divine one" (GS 22).

Thus we grow in the spirit of our withdrawal from society by handing over to God all our energy and abilities, by bringing to completion our conversion of heart, submitting all our being, our interests, and our desires to the will of Christ, so that they may be purified and transformed by His Spirit.

This is really just the spirituality of the *beatitudes*, which are the primary expressions of the new law of love, so opposed to the ideals of this world—poverty, meekness, suffering, justice, purity, etc. These values and inner attitudes are precisely the distinctive signs of the religious vocation: "Religious, by their state in life, give splendid and striking testimony that the world cannot be transfigured and offered to God without the spirit of the beatitudes" (LG 31).

Purity of Heart

"Going to the Father" and "leaving the world" imply "leaving *things*." If the monk leaves the things of the world it is not because they are bad, but because they impede him in his paschal journey with Christ to the kingdom of heaven. They are good, but for the moment he cannot use them because his heart, his love, *is not pure.* When we are full of self-love, creatures contribute to our ruin. But when we are purified by grace, then creatures help us to love God: "Blest are the single-hearted for they shall see God" (Mt. 5:8) The difficulty is not in things but in us.

So what matters most in the vow of conversion of life is purity of heart—the *renouncement of myself,* with its correlative, the *love of Christ,* and both of these realities blossoming into a spontaneous *compassion for my brother.* This is the purpose of all our observances and austerities. We can renounce everything in the world and follow the monastic observances with exactitude, but it will profit us nothing without the renouncement of ourselves. In fact, the observances will do us much harm, rooting in us the most dangerous form of pride.

The practical conclusion is obvious—the importance of *humility*. Not without reason Saint Benedict makes the life of the monk revolve around this fundamental disposition of heart. Purity of love comes in the footsteps of inner humility, as we shall see in more detail when we discuss spiritual methods in Chapter Seven: "Having climbed all these degrees of humility, the monk will soon arrive at that love of God which, being perfect, casts out all fear" (RB 7, 67).

If the body of conversion of life consists in the essential monastic observances—solitude, silence, lectio divina, austerity of life, common life, work, and the like—its soul is found in Christian humility. The body is necessary, but without the soul it is of little value. Besides, just as the human soul does not spring forth automatically from the body, but must come from without by a special creation of God, so also the observances merely form a favorable environment in which to receive the Spirit of God. The spirit of monastic life, this spirit of humility and love, *is the Spirit Himself of Christ, the Holy Spirit, working in the heart of the monk*, leading him to the desert, purifying him, and raising him to the Father. The vow of conversion is a vow to live "in the Spirit."

The monastic spirit, then, is nothing other than the special mode of action of the Spirit of Christ in the person who gives himself fully to the observances of our life. On the other hand, the Holy Spirit will express Himself in the life of the monk by a free and serene *fidelity* to these observances. And above all by love for the brethren: "We know that we have passed from death to life, because we love the brethren. He who does not love remains in death" (I Jn. 3:14).

This love, in its turn, is expressed in works. The good works of RB 4 are so many expressions of conversion of life, and all of RB 72 on good zeal is a perfect summary of the spirit of conversion according to monastic tradition. Purity of heart is nothing else but an operative fullness of the love of Christ.

Transformation in Christ

In the last analysis, the vow of conversion has a transforming character. An inner spiritual transformation is implied in its relation to the paschal mystery and in its orientation to purity of heart. This is why the monk's *conversatio*, or objective way of life, is ultimately subordinated to his *conversio*, his subjective conversion to Christ. The monk's vocation is to sound the depths of Christian conversion, the primary exigency of the Gospel. We shall see in Chapter Seven how monastic humility pinpoints this exigency and responds to it.

Saint Paul sums up what this process of conversion consists in: "Do not conform yourselves to this age but be transformed by the renewal of your mind, so that you may judge what is God's will" (Rom. 12:2).

We separate ourselves physically from the world, we follow Christ into the desert, we embrace the monastic observances and the life of prayer, we give ourselves permanently to a common life of poverty and fraternal love only to make ourselves more like Jesus Christ, to have His thoughts, His desires, His aspirations and sentiments. Cassian presents this traditional monastic doctrine with all clarity in Conference 10, 7: the model for monastic conversion is Christ's union with the Father, "so that your love for me may live in them, and I may live in them" (Jn. 17:26).

This living in Christ and Christ in the monk is the definitive "manner of life" (*conversatio*) implied by our vow. Diagram I on the next page helps to bring out this internal dynamism of conversion and sum up what we have tried to say throughout this chapter. It is based on the different interrelated stages of *conversatio* and *conversio*.

All this dynamism of conversion and new life is what we embrace on the day of profession. It is an ascetic life, but above all it is a life of transformation in Christ. It is a journey, and the principal factor of any journey is its destination. Our goal is "to see in His kingdom Him who called us" (RB Prol., 21), which implies a transformation: "All of us, with faces uncovered, reflecting as in a mirror the glory of the Lord, are being transformed into His image" (II Cor. 3:18).

What does this transformation mean? Is it something mystical?

Yes, the spirit of our vow of conversion of life is *to desire and to aspire to a mystical transformation in Christ.* Not in order to be better than other men nor to believe ourselves superior to others by our grade of sanctity, but simply because Christ died and rose again precisely for this. This is why we were baptized:

Through baptism into his death we were buried with him, so that, just as Christ was raised from the dead by the glory of the Father, we too might live a new life (Rom. 6:4).

The life I live now is not my own: Christ is living in me. I still live my human life, but it is a life of faith in the Son of God, who loved me and gave himself for me (Gal. 2:20).

Diagram I.

CONVERSION OF LIFE ACCORDING TO
BENEDICTINE-CISTERCIAN SPIRITUALITY

I. *Conversatio saeculi:* the manner of life in the world, which easily
    (cf. RB 4, 20)   brings with it a division of spirit (I Cor. 7).

By an external conversion
the Christian embraces the   (=the external renunciations)
monastic life.

II. *Conversatio morum:*   the new manner of life in the monastery;
    (RB 58, 17)   the basic observances.

By an interior conversion
of heart, the monk becomes
more "rational" and "spirit-   (=the internal and moral
ual," growing in the values   renunciations; the use
which correspond to the   of the spiritual art)
exterior observances,
especially faith, humility
and love: *purity of heart*.

III. *Conversatio in caelis:* the new life of identification with Christ
     (Phil. 3:20)   characteristic of the kingdom of heaven;
                              docility to the Spirit; continual prayer.
                              (=the contemplative renunciations)

The life of Christ is poured into the believers, who, through the sacraments, are united in a hidden and real way to Christ who suffered and was glorified. ...All the members ought to be molded into Christ's image until He is formed in them. For this reason we who have been made like unto Him, who have died with Him and been raised up with Him, are taken up into the mysteries of His life (LG 7).

Through the institution of the monastic life God has willed to call to Himself men in whose poverty He can freely manifest the glory of His grace and the greatness of His mercy to those who are in Christ Jesus. To let God transform our nothingness into the image of His Son is not pride. It is plain gratitude for the grace of our vocation.

For Further Reflection

1. When you entered the monastic life were you more aware of its active aspect or of its contemplative dimension? Which is the dominant factor for you at present?

2. Of the five basic observances treated in this chapter, which seems to be the most important one for you? And for your community? Which is the least important?

3. Is there such a thing as what is commonly called "religious perfection"? What would "monastic perfection" be? In what does perfection essentially consist?

Bibliography

FOR "CONVERSATIO" IN RB:

Colombas, G., et al. *San Benito, su vida y su Regla*. Madrid: BAC 115, 1968, pp. 752-761.
de Vogue, A. *La Regle de Saint Benoit*, Vol. VI, pp. 1324-1329.
McCann, J. *The Rule of St. Benedict*. London: Burns and Oates, 1952, pp. 168, 196, 202-208.
Peifer, C. *Monastic Spirituality*, pp. 303-306.
Rees, D., et al. *Consider Your Call*, pp. 144-146.
Schmitz, P. "Conversatio morum," in *Dictionnaire de Spiritualité*, T. 2. Paris: Beauchesne, 1953, cc. 2206-2211.
Steidle, B. *The Rule of St. Benedict*, pp. 254-256.

ON MONASTIC OBSERVANCES AND THEIR SPIRIT:

Bouyer, L. *Introduction to Spirituality*. New York: Desclee, 1961, pp. 185-212.
_____. *The Meaning of the Monastic Life*. New York: Kenedy, 1955.
Chadwick, O. *John Cassian*. Cambridge: Univ. Press, (2nd ed.), 1968.

Deseille, P. *Principes de spiritualite monastique.* Begrolles: Abbaye de Bellefontaine, 1974, esp. pp. 55-94.

―――. *Regards sur la tradition monastique.* Begrolles: Abbaye de Bellefontaine, 1974, esp. pp. 83-155.

de H. Doherty, C. *Poustinia.* Notre Dame: Ave Maria Press, 1975.

Evdokimov, P. *The Struggle With God.* Glen Rock, New Jersey: Paulist Press, 1966.

Maloney, G. A. *Russian Hesychasm: The Spirituality of Nil Sorskij.* The Hague: Mouton, 1973, esp. pp. 103-172.

Merton, T. *Contemplation in a World of Action.* Garden City: Doubleday, 1971, pp. 98-165 and 237-330.

―――. *The Monastic Journey.* Kansas City: Sheed and Ward; London: Sheldon Press, 1977.

―――. *The Silent Life.* New York: Farrar, Straus, 1957.

Peifer, C. *Monastic Spirituality,* pp. 192-246 and 307-312.

Rees, D., et al. *Consider Your Call,* pp. 94-109, 147-153, and 301-317.

Regamey, P., et al. *Redecouverte du jeune.* Paris: Cerf, 1959.

Region of the Isles, *Symposium on the Vows,* pp. F14-J14, (studies on "conversatio morum").

Theologie de la vie monastique. Paris: Aubier, 1961, esp. pp. 15-38, 213-240, and 503-540.

Ward, B., trans. *The Sayings of the Fathers of the Desert: The Alphabetical Collection,* CS 59. London: Mowbray; Kalamazoo: Cistercian Publications, 1975.

Wathen, A. G. *Silence,* CS 22, 1973.

ON MONASTIC PRAYER, LECTIO DIVINA, AND THE DIVINE OFFICE:

Abhishiktananda (Fr. H. Le Saux). *Prayer.* London: SPCK; Philadelphia: Westminster Press, 1967.

Anonymous. *The Cloud of Unknowing and The Book of Privy Counseling.* Edited by W. Johnston. Garden City: Doubleday Image, 1973.

―――. *The Way of a Pilgrim.* Translated by R. M. French. London: SPCK, 1960.

Bamberger, J. E. "Introduction," in Evagrius Ponticus, *The Praktikos, Chapters on Prayer,* CS 4, pp. xxiii-11.

Bouyer, L. *Introduction to Spirituality,* pp. 1-124 and 261-310.

―――. *Liturgical Piety.* Notre Dame. Indiana: Univ. of N. D. Press, 1955, esp. pp. 185-271.

Cassian, J. *The Conferences IX-X,* (on prayer), The Nicene and Post-Nicene Fathers, op. cit., pp. 387-409.

Chapman, J. *Spiritual Letters of Abbot Chapman.* London: Sheed and Ward, 1946.

Deseille, P. *Principes de spiritualite monastique,* pp. 35-54 and 95-114 .

Evagrius Ponticus. *The Praktikos, Chapters on Prayer,* CS 4, pp. 12-80.

Hausherr, I. *Hesychasme et Priere.* Rome: Pont. Inst. Orientalium Studiorum, 1966.

―――. *Adorer le Pere en Esprit et en Verite.* Paris: Lethielleux, 1967.

―――. *Priere de vie, vie de priere.* Paris: Lethielleux, 1965.

Higgins, J. *Merton's Theology of Prayer,* CS 18, 1971, published subsequently as *Thomas Merton on Prayer.* Garden City: Doubleday, 1971.

Johnston, W. *Christian Zen.* New York: Harper and Row, 1972.

―――. *Silent Music: The Science of Meditation.* New York: Harper and Row, 1974, esp. pp. 53-140.

―――. *The Mysticism of the Cloud of Unknowing.* St. Meinrad, Indiana: Abbey Press, 1975.

_____. *The Still Point: Reflections on Zen and Christian Mysticism*. New York: Harper and Row, 1971.

Kadloubovsky, E. and Palmer, G. L., translators of the following three works published by Faber and Faber, London:

_____. *Writings from the Philokalia on Prayer of the Heart*, 1951.

_____. *Early Fathers from the Philokalia*, 1954.

_____. *The Art of Prayer: An Orthodox Anthology*, 1966.

Leclercq, J. *The Love of Learning and the Desire for God*. New York: Fordham Univ. Press, 1960, esp. pp. 16-21 and 89-91.

Loew, J. *Face to Face with God*. New York: Paulist Press, 1977, esp. pp. 126-141.

Louf, A. *Teach us to Pray*. London: Darton, Longman and Todd, 1974; Chicago: Franciscan Herald Press, 1975; Ramsey, New Jersey: Paulist Press, 1977.

Martin, R. *Hungry for God*. New York: Doubleday, 1974.

Merton, T. *Bread in the Wilderness*. New York: New Directions, 1953.

_____. *Contemplation in a World of Action*, esp. pp. 331-384.

_____. *The Climate of Monastic Prayer*, CS 1, 1969, subsequently published as *Contemplative Prayer*. Garden City: Doubleday Image, 1969.

_____. *New Seeds of Contemplation*. New York: New Directions, 1961.

_____. *Opening the Bible*. New York: New Directions, 1973.

_____. *Praying the Psalms*. Collegeville, Minnesota: Liturgical Press, 1956.

_____. *Seasons of Celebration*. New York: Farrar, Straus, 1965.

Monk of the Eastern Church. *Jesus: A Dialogue with the Saviour*. New York: Desclee, 1965; Glen Rock, New Jersey: Paulist Press, 1965.

_____. *On the Invocation of the Name of Jesus*. London: Fellowship of St. Alban and St. Sergius, 1970.

_____. *The Prayer of Jesus*. New York: Desclee, 1967.

Muto, S. A. *Approaching the Sacred: An Introduction to Spiritual Reading*. Denville, New Jersey: Dimension Books, 1973.

Peifer, C. *Monastic Spirituality*, pp. 384-470.

Pennington, B. *Daily We Touch Him*. Garden City: Doubleday, 1977.

_____., ed. *One Yet Two*, CS 29, 1976, pp. 22-47 and 304-351.

Raguin, Y. *Chemins de la contemplation*. Tournai: Desclee, 1969.

Rees, D., et al. *Consider Your Call*, pp. 221-300.

Rinker, R. *Prayer: Conversing with God*. Grand Rapids, Michigan: Zondervan Books, 1975.

Superiors' and Novice Masters' Meeting, (on continual prayer). Conyers, Georgia: Holy Spirit Abbey, mimeographed, 1976.

von Balthasar, H. U. *Prayer*. New York: Sheed and Ward, 1961.

CHAPTER THREE

CONSECRATED CHASTITY

It is significant that Saint Benedict does not refer to this promise of chastity in his chapter on monastic profession (RB 58). When the monk pronounces his vows, the words *chastity* or *virginity* are not even mentioned.

Why is this so?

Above all, because of the evident necessity of such a condition for a life totally dedicated "to the love of Christ...keeping stability in the monastic family" (RB 4). A promise of chastity is so fundamental that you cannot conceive the monastic state without it. Its absence in the traditional profession formula implies that consecrated chastity is included in the vow of conversion of life.

1. MEANING OF CONSECRATED VIRGINITY

Its Importance

Just as it is hard to think of a blind man driving a truck in the center of a modern city, so also it would be very difficult to imagine monastic life without a promise of chastity. The Rule reflects this fact in speaking of poverty:

> Let no one presume to give or receive anything without permission of the abbot, or to have anything of his own...since they are not permitted to have even their bodies or wills at their own disposal (RB 33, 2-4).

Saint Benedict refers here to a personal relation like that which exists between a married couple: "A wife does not belong to herself but to her husband. In the same way, the husband does not belong to himself, but to his wife" (I Cor. 7:4). The thought seems to be that the monk has entered into a marital relation, not only with God but also with the community of which he is a member. This relation of mutual love and duties is so fundamental that it hardly needs explanation, and the Rule refers to it as to something obvious to all concerned.

The mentality shown here in the Rule reflects a traditional attitude which was common in the first centuries of Christianity, but which was lost sight of during many centuries and is only now entering again into Christian spirituality. The difference of approach can be seen by the fact that, since the Middle Ages until very recently, it was customary to enumerate the three religious vows according to the hierarchy of goods sacrificed to God. There was a progress from those of lesser value to those of greater worth:

-sacrifice of exterior material goods by *poverty*
-sacrifice of the goods of one's own body by *chastity*
-sacrifice of the good of one's own will by *obedience*

At times the order was inverted, starting with obedience, because of its more universal influence in the organized religious life. Then came poverty, and finally chastity as the least influential in daily life.

Nevertheless, in point of fact the most radical vow is that of chastity or *consecrated virginity*. Thus the Decree of Vatican II on the religious life treats of chastity *before* poverty and obedience, as also is done in the Constitution on the Church in speaking of the Gospel counsels:

Outstanding among the manifold counsels proposed in the Gospel by our Lord to His disciples is that precious gift of divine grace which the Father gives to some men so that by virginity, or celibacy, they can more easily devote their entire selves to God alone with undivided heart (LG 42).

Central Element of the Life of the Vows

The Church thus returned to an approach shown by the Gospels and the First Letter to the Corinthians. When Jesus referred to a special dedication to the kingdom of God, He did so in terms of chastity, using the concrete language typical of His semitic culture:

Not everyone can accept this teaching, only those to whom it is given to do so.... There are eunuchs who have made themselves that way for the sake of the kingdom of heaven. Let anyone accept this who can (Mt. 19:11-12).

The children of this world take wives and husbands, but those judged worthy of a place in the world to come and of resurrection from the dead do not. They become like angels and are no longer subject to death. Sons of resurrection, they are sons of God (Lk. 20:34-35).

Saint Paul shows that the words of Jesus refer both to a future life and to the present, by applying the same teaching to a concrete situation:

I want you to be free of all worries. The unmarried man is busy with the Lord's affairs and concerned with pleasing Him, whereas the married man is busy with this world's demands and occupied with pleasing his wife. This means that he is divided.... I am going into this with you for your own good. I have no desire to place restrictions on you, but I do want to promote what is good, what will help you devote yourselves entirely to the Lord (I Cor. 7:32-35).

These counsels of Jesus to His disciples and of Paul to the first Christians ought to make us live our vow of chastity with joy and enthusiasm. It is the *central element* in the life of those who, following the call of Christ, leave everything in order "to devote themselves entirely to the Lord." When it is lived correctly, chastity will produce a liberation in love.

Occasionally Jesus' words concerning the renunciation of marriage are interpreted as referring more to marital chastity than to a state of non-marriage. But even if this were the case, it would not weaken the Christian meaning of consecrated virginity, which is based on an inner movement of the Spirit more than on any particular text of the Gospel. Christian tradition has been a constant witness to this lived interpretation of Christ's words and the desire to imitate His virginal way of life.

Thus from the primitive Church until the twelfth century, consecrated virginity was fully accepted as an official state of life which was independent of the profession of poverty or obedience. Both by its inner demands and through its social structure of non-marriage, consecrated virginity continues to be the element which most tangibly separates the religious from the bonds of this world. For a monk, we can say that all the other elements of his profession spring from this one.

Note on Terminology

A clarification of the words *chastity* and *virginity* will be a first step to help us enter into the full meaning of our vow. In this sense, it seems that the phrase *consecrated virginity* is the most adequate term to express the content of the vow of "chastity." We have used both terms until now because the word *chastity* is more common and is the one used in the Decree of Vatican II on religious life (PC 12).

Chastity has a very broad meaning. It is the correct attitude in respect to sexuality in general. It is that part of the virtue of temperance which controls and orients everything concerned with the sexual instinct— thoughts, desires, acts, pleasures, etc., both within married life and outside of it. Chastity is ordered, like sexuality itself, to marriage or to virginity.

> Chastity should be practiced by people according to their different states of life. Some will live it in virginity or consecrated celibacy, which is an outstanding way of giving oneself more easily, with an undivided heart, to God alone. Others will live it according to the dictates of Christian morality, either in marriage or as celibates (PH 11).

Perfect chastity consists in abstaining from the sexual act. It implies total continence, with the intention of keeping this continence in the future. Such abstention can even be practiced in the marriage state for various reasons. Similarly, the vow of *celibacy*, in the sense of a promise not to marry, can be made for very noble reasons, without necessarily being a response to the call of Christ, e.g., in order better to exercise a profession, to care for the sick, etc.

Virginity has a more precise meaning and seems to express more exactly the specifically Christian content of our vow. It reflects an essential element in the invitation of Jesus: the renouncement of marriage ("making oneself a eunuch," "not marrying") *for love of Christ*, that is to say, to follow Him and imitate Him ("for the sake of the kingdom of heaven," "in the world to come and of resurrection from the dead," "to devote yourselves entirely to the Lord").

The election and profession of chastity has to be made directly for God, without any other end in view than to belong to God in a special way. It is not enough to accept it as approved by God. Chastity ought to be ordered to Him much more directly—it is *consecrated* to God. This state has an element of mystery. Not all understand it nor will understand it. It belongs to the world to come. It causes us to enter even now into the liberty of a risen body. It testifies to the definitive and eternal state of every Christian.

The word *virginity* is more apt for expressing this content of the vow which is not only spiritual but also supernatural and eschatological—a consecration in body and soul to the exclusive love of Christ which springs from a movement of the Holy Spirit in the heart of the Christian.

We understand by the word *virginity* not only the material or natural virginity of those who preserve corporal integrity, but also virginity "recovered" in some way by penitence, and even Christian widowhood. *The promise of perpetual abstinence* is the principal element. That which is consecrated by the vow of conversion of life is the present and the future, not the past.

Christian virginity, or consecrated virginity, thus signifies two things: the *state* of perpetual abstinence from marriage, and the *consecration*, or inner dedication, of this state to Christ.

2. BASIC REQUIREMENTS

With greater clarity concerning the meaning of consecrated virginity, we can now approach its fundamental demands. In this vow, more than in any other, the interior, psychological, and spiritual aspects receive principal attention. In fact, it is impossible to separate this interiority of Christian chastity from its more external dimensions, since, for the person who is living the vow, "the virtue of chastity is not limited to the avoidance of sexual disorders. It has other higher and more positive demands, for it is a virtue which marks the whole personality, both interiorly and exteriorly" (PH 11). This breadth of chastity's action will become evident in what follows.

State of Consecrated Virginity

In the first place, there is the call to interior fidelity to the state of virginity, which implies the *renunciation of any thought or desire of marriage.*

By vowing consecrated virginity, we promise to renounce not only the pleasure which always comes with the use of the sexual organs (which every unmarried Christian must renounce), but also the very possibility of matrimony. For a person without vows there is no sin in thinking about or arranging his life for marriage. On the contrary, it is good and pleasing to the Lord. But for a religious to think seriously and with deliberation about getting married, even without thinking of sexual acts or pleasure, would be a real infidelity to Jesus and to the chastity which he has promised.

Such a marriage contracted by a religious in solemn vows is not only gravely illicit but invalid in the eyes of the Church.

Cultivation of Chastity

The vow, however, is ordered to the practice of chastity on a higher level, as a consequence of a definitive consecration of both body and soul to Jesus Christ. Although human nature itself is ordered to this deeper growth in chastity, and baptism inserts this growth into the mystery of Christ, the celibate state fosters it in a very special way. Religious profession explicitates this celibacy on a permanent basis and relates it publicly to the Person of Christ.

This signifies, in a negative way, the renunciation of any voluntary act directly ordered to sexual (i.e., genital) stimulation and pleasure. An infidelity in this matter would tend to have a double gravity, for it would be contrary to chastity in itself, and would also go against the promise made publicly to God.

But this negative obligation receives its weight from chastity's positive meaning. The vow signifies, above all, that you assume responsibility of cultivating chastity positively. What does this mean?

Chastity means integrating your sexuality into the rest of your human, Christian, and monastic life. There are two general, simultaneous phases to this process. First, *becoming aware* of your sexuality, that you are made to love, and that you have an indelible mark on all levels of your human and Christian love, which is intimately related to the sex given to you by God. Then comes the gradual *inner ordering* of these levels of love, so that all the life energy which God has granted you can be expressed in a way which corresponds to your total vocation as a son of God in Christ Jesus.

This is the real work of chastity, a life-long process which will really not be completed until your entire being is glorified on the day of the final resurrection. Yet this transformation of sexual love can and should begin to take place in this life, thanks to the inner virtue of chastity, which is a very real force infused by the Holy Spirit into your heart, mind, and body. The vow is directly ordered to this inner work of chastity, because

> chastity can in no case be reduced to mere exterior behavior. It should purify man's heart, according to Christ's words: "You have heard it said that you shall not commit adultery. But I say to you that he who looks with desire on a woman has already committed adultery with her in his heart" (PH 11).

There has been much literature written on this subject, from both the psychological and the religious points of view. In the following paragraphs we shall simply develop the most basic points contained in the two general, simultaneous phases mentioned above.

HUMAN SEXUALITY

Sexuality is one of the principal factors in human existence. It goes far beyond, or underneath, the reproductive phenomena and gives a masculine or feminine characteristic to every cell of the human body. All human action, thought, growth, and especially the different forms of human love are conditioned by it, since man expresses what he is above all by his loves.

> According to contemporary science, the human person is marked by his or her sexuality in such a way that it is to be considered one of the principal elements which go to make up man's life. In fact the typical features which constitute persons as men or women on the biological, psychological, and spiritual levels are rooted in their sex. Sexuality thus plays an important role in the individual's personal maturity and in his insertion into society (PH 1).

In itself, sexuality is an inner structure or sector of human existence which expresses the dramatic situation of man as being both spiritual and animal. It reveals, principally in our emotional plane but also in our bodily organs and our spiritual desires, the disproportion which exists between the finite and the infinite, between our material body and our divine vocation. Thus sexuality becomes a place of tension and conflict, in a way which other sectors of our existence, such as intelligence and will, do not. But is also becomes a beautiful meeting place for all creation, a place of living and loving synthesis between the animal instincts and the spiritual openness which characterizes human life. Such a synthesis is seen in the saints, in that fruit of purity of heart which Christian orthodox spirituality calls "universal tenderness." It is the sweetness and the compassionate strength of the sons of God.

Sexuality, then, is a gift from God which, at one and the same time, makes the human race bisexual and acts as a centrifugal force that opens our bodies, our minds, and our hearts to others, precisely as different from ourselves. It makes a person capable of a specific type of love (masculine or feminine) even in his relation to God. It gives a specific shape or color to his or her innate drive toward personal union with the "other" and to the repose in such union once achieved. Moreover each particular person has his own concrete sexuality, a particular blend of instinct, openness, masculinity, femininity, and intensity.

This more general and dynamic vision of sexuality in no way implies explaining everything in terms of sex ("pansexualism"), but it does show the need for a proper use of words and a modification of certain ways of thinking. For example, it is a mistake to say that by the vow of consecrated virginity one "gives up sex" if we mean by this that we give up sexuality. What we give up is the very limited sphere of voluntary acts directly ordered to genital stimulation and pleasure. There remain the less exciting physiological aspects of sex, together with the entire psychological and spiritual process of reordering our "sexed" personality and centering it on Christ. In this sense, the renunciation of stimulation *helps* sex, since it orders it to its true goal. Sexuality is a responsibility, a task, and chastity fosters this task.

The close relation between sexuality and the rest of human life, especially human love, means that chastity will express itself in different ways according to how we live and how we love. Growth in chastity will imply passing from an infantile, egocentric love centered on bodily and emotional self-satisfaction, to a stable, mature attitude of oblative self-giving centered in the other person. A normal element in this growth process is a healthy, positive, yet sober relation toward the other sex.

In this connection, it is helpful to see how there are *four kinds of love* which continually interact in every sincere person's life. Sexuality, and therefore chastity, express themselves on all four levels. The predominance of one or another type of love will determine the degree of affective maturity and of growth in chastity:

-physical love, *sex*, or sex appeal

-sensitive love, or *eros*

-brotherly love, or friendship (*philia*)

-divine love, charity, or *agape*

Christian chastity has for its task the proper ordering of these inner forces. It will avoid an artificial repression of the lower levels of human love, and will rather orient them by directing their sexual energy toward its true center and destiny, the love of Christ, *agape*.

CHRIST AND CHASTITY

We have already seen how the vow of conversion of life is ordered to a real inner transformation in Christ through love. Consecrated virginity makes this orientation explicit. The life of the risen Jesus, which is in the center of your soul through baptism, gives you this new force of unity and integration, far stronger than any merely psychological technique. Its influence on the levels of sexuality is something like the work of a rolling snowball which assumes new layers of snow around its center, like a magnet establishing an ordered field of energy around itself, or like the yeast which makes the whole dough rise (Mt. 13:33). This is why the cultivation of chastity must start with real love for Jesus Christ, much more than from a mere discipline of physical love.

So *the secret center of chastity is love of Jesus and of His Virgin Mother*. This means a manly tenderness, full of admiration for the perfect human nature of Christ and for the immaculate fidelity of Mary. It means imitating their example and filling our thoughts with their own thoughts.

The life of consecrated virginity frees our human affectivity and loosens our emotions from many natural objects which are normally associated with the different levels of human love and sexuality. These renunciations refer to goods that are profoundly engraved in our heart and in our flesh. They offer to the Lord the legitimate desires of human love, paternity, affection, and all the values which these realities bring with them, as we shall see in the following pages.

All this affective force must be oriented and led to the person of Jesus Christ. To bind oneself to Jesus by a vow of consecrated virginity involves the intelligence, the emotions, and the will. It is the work of many years, but with a life of authentic prayer and generosity, it is achieved naturally and spontaneously. Sexual love, human tenderness, and friendships are inserted into the love of Christ and are transformed by it. There they find their true meaning which, however, often does not appear until after the process has taken place. This can be seen in the following experience of one of the Desert Mothers:

The spirit of fornication once attacked Amma Sarah with more than the usual insistence, reminding her of the vanities of the world. But she gave herself up to the fear of God and to asceticism and went up onto her little terrace to pray. Then the spirit of fornication appeared corporally to her and said, "Sarah, you have overcome me." But she said, "It is not I who have overcome you, but my master, Christ."

With this primacy of divine love firmly in mind, we can look briefly now at how Christian chastity works on the other levels of our sexuality.

CHASTITY AND SENSUALITY

The most rudimentary level of sexuality is that of physical love, which involves man's entire body with special reference to the reproductive organs and their functions, since it is through them that corporal self-donation is felt and expressed with maximum intensity. By religious profession, we give up, in total love of Christ, certain acts directly related to this dimension of human love, as has been specified above.

Related in practice to biological sex is the vice of sensuality, an habitual indulgence of the senses in matters which border on the sexual sphere, especially in relation to the senses of touch and sight. Consecrated virginity will resist this tendency of our sexuality to concentrate on the corporal, physiological, or sensual aspects of sex. It will discipline the body so as to make it an apt companion and instrument of the soul, a worthy temple of the Holy Spirit. In this connection, we should avoid always seeking the most comfortable postures, the tastiest foods, etc.

At the same time, it is an important part of chastity to treat the body as something consecrated, which it is. We should do our reasonable best to maintain our body clean and in good health. Sensuality is the vice which seeks the pleasures of the senses, which are good in themselves, in order to satisfy us on the level of physical love without relation to the love of Christ. Chastity, on the other hand, directs our senses and all our being to the Word made flesh, and to His love in us. Modesty of dress has its role to play here.

Is it possible for a religious to flee excessively from this biological level of his sexuality? Yes, this seems to have been somewhat common in recent centuries and to have provoked a series of ridiculous taboos in religious communities and seminaries. On the social level, it resulted in strict segregation of the sexes. Monastic enclosure, of course, lent itself to such segregation and sometimes has fostered an immature attitude toward the opposite sex based more on a fear of sexuality than on an inner sobriety of spirit. The reception of mixed groups and the avoidance of sexual discrimination can prove healthy in this regard if it is done with discretion and respect for the norms of enclosure.

On this more primitive level of sexuality, then, chastity will avoid the two extremes of sensuality and prudishness. By so doing, it will integrate bodily sexuality into the overall flow of Christian life, begin to open the person to others, and initiate the construction of a community based on a higher love.

CHASTITY AND EROS

The complex drive of our human nature toward self-fulfillment and self-transcendence constitutes what can be called "sensitive love," or what the Greeks called "eros." It is the *central dimension of human sexuality* but not its goal, although contemporary western culture may give that impression. Nor is it limited exclusively to "erotic love," or to "erotism," which is the perversion of true sensitivity and refers more to lust.

Eros is rather the psychological level of human love. Its most typical form of expression is affection or tenderness towards a member of the other sex. But it can also be oriented to a person of the same sex (normally in friendship and abnormally in homosexuality), toward oneself (autoerotism or narcissism), or channeled into activities such as sports, love of animals, hobbies, or creative work. This inner drive toward self-fulfillment accounts for man's love of the beauties of creation, his dedication to the fine arts, to the love of knowledge, and even to religious values such as devotion, worship, and asceticism.

Eros is thus the energetic aspect of human sexuality, which expresses itself in a multitude of ways and thus becomes the link between physical love and spiritual love. The result, of course, is that eros is often a battleground between these two other types of love, which seek to harness for their own use the vital energy contained in this center of man's sexuality. All forms of spirituality are witnesses, in one way or another, to this battle:

> Abba Gerontios of Petra said that many, tempted by the pleasures of the body, commit fornication, not in their body but in their spirit, and while preserving their bodily virginity, commit prostitution in their soul. "Thus it is good, my well-beloved, to do that which is written, and for each one to guard his own heart with all possible care" (Prov. 4:23).

> A brother asked Abba Poemen, "What shall I do, for fornication and anger war against me?" The old man said, "In this connection David said: 'I will

pierce the lion and I will slay the bear'; that is to say: I will cut off anger and I will crush fornication with hard labor."

Such education and discipline of our sensitive feelings is the classical field of action for the virtue of chastity. It is noteworthy that in the latter apophtegma of Abba Poemen, it is anger that is "cut off," whereas fornication is destroyed by directing its energy into "hard labor," i.e., manual work. This points to the fact that by our vow of chastity we do not, and cannot, really "give up" eros as a reality in itself, but only insofar as it is taken as the norm of human life. In fact, chastity *strengthens* eros so that it can more fully serve the deeper and more spiritual levels of love.

But just *how* does chastity work on the emotions? Chastity usually works best in an atmosphere which combines the confidence of brotherly love with the austerity of the desert experience. In the desert our sensitive love is purified like a precious metal, in what is called by Saint John of the Cross the "dark nights," and by Saint Benedict the "steps of humility" (RB 7). The process implies a reorganization of our inner life energy which can only be accomplished by God Himself. It is what Cassian called "purity of heart" (Conf. 1, 5-11).

Benedictine-Cistercian spirituality offers a complete life-program as a supporting context to help this renewal of our sexuality in inner imitation of Christ. We shall summarize this spirituality more adequately in a future chapter, but even now we can see that its different elements are meant to take hold of our senses and feelings and orient them toward a balanced form of expression in accord with God's plan to "reorganize all things in Christ" (Eph. 1:10).

Consecrated virginity will express itself through these different means and give the whole monastic project an inner intensity which would otherwise be lacking. It will praise the Lord for the fact that the often wearisome journey of chastity is not just a question of self-mastery, but of Jesus-mastery.

This is especially so in those spheres of sensitive love where the specific characteristics of the different sexes are most evident. Man's greater orientation to *things or ideas* and woman's stronger emphasis on *persons*, man's search to dominate and to influence others through possessing or controlling them and woman's skill in influencing others by being possessed by them, the masculine tendency to obstinate force and the feminine tendency to obstinate sentimentality, all these expressions of eros often become stronger with the years. The masculine and feminine poles of gravity coexist and can even reinforce each other in any one person.

In this erotic search for power, monastic life only offers a frustratingly limited scope for achievement, since it is fundamentally an imitation of Christ's self-emptying. Yet thanks to this frustration of self-will, our more aggressive impulses and self-centered ideas are educated, then dominated by the Spirit of Jesus, who makes use of both joy and sorrow to accomplish His work.

The celibate life itself, when lived in the light of Christ, is a powerful aid to such maturation of human love. This becomes evident on the more spiritual levels of our affective life.

Chastity and Friendship

The third level of sexuality is that of brotherly love corresponding to the Greek work, *philia*. This is true interpersonal love and adds to physical love and sensitive love the spiritual qualities of altruism, generosity, and loyalty. Whereas eros is more an inner drive toward self-fulfillment, friendship forgets self in its emphasis on the person loved. The dedicated love between members of the same family is often a good example of this altruism which also appears in the love for one's country, one's community, or the poor. Conjugal love itself, if it is to be lasting, must have a greater share of friendship to it than mere sensitive love or biological sex. Friendship's supreme act, as Jesus said, is to "lay down one's life" for the person loved (Jn. 15:13).

An openness to friendship and to healthy interpersonal relations is extremely important in monastic life, but not as easy as it sounds. It implies a real cenobitic asceticism of humility, patience, sincerity, and clarity of communication—which does not necessarily mean a lot of speaking. Such an attitude is at the root of Saint Benedict's steps of humility and good zeal (RB 7 and 72): "The brothers are also to obey one another, knowing that by this road of obedience they will go to God" (RB 71, 1). He reflects here a strong tradition in cenobitic and semi-eremitic monasticism which had already found expression in Pachomian spirituality and in Cassian's teaching on monastic friendship (Conf. 16). Abba Theonas' attitude is another example:

> Abba Poemen quoted Abba Theonas as saying, "Even if a man acquires a virtue, God does not grant him grace for himself alone." He knew that he was not faithful in his own labor, but that if he went to his companion, God would be with him.

Yet experience repeatedly shows how easy it is to fall into extremes in this matter of brotherly love. On the one hand, friendship (*philia*) must be continually purified by divine love (*agape*) in order not to degenerate into the sentimentality of *eros* or the carnal tension of physical love.

Such purification will be the first work of chastity on this beautiful new level of human affection.

What is at stake here is the whole problem of "particular friendships" which, since brotherly love is by nature particular, would be better called "exclusive friendships."

Such relations involve a preoccupation with one particular person to the detriment of other interpersonal relations. Instead of purifying our feelings by the light of Christ, they stunt our growth by a certain emotional infatuation. We should talk over such a situation with our spiritual guide, or at least with some mature person who can help us elaborate it and discover its roots within ourselves.

Intimate friendship presupposes a certain maturity of spirit. It is a delicate flower of brotherly love and should not be striven after as though it were necessary for spiritual growth. It is more common and generally healthier that the monk or nun experience more solitude than fraternal intimacy. Solitude can often open us up in greater joy and simplicity to the lasting friendship of Christ. Experience teaches that the virtues of generosity and loyalty, mixed with a sense of reverence for the mystery of our brothers, are clearer landmarks of Christian *philia* than is a search for a tender friend.

But on the other hand, it is easy in practice to go to the other extreme and shy away from fraternal intimacy when a brother is sincerely looking for help along his way to God. Saint Aelred of Rievaulx, the twelfth century English Cistercian, put down some useful guidelines on this matter in his classic treatise *On Spiritual Friendship*. Aelred's central message is that Christ is present as a third party in Christian friendship, as He Himself promised in Mt. 18:20. The gaze of friends is drawn toward Him, yet they remain ever more closely united, one to another, like the disciples of Emmaus (Lk. 24:32). It is Christ Himself, in the power of His resurrection, who frees friendship from the pull of self-satisfaction and sentimentality, drawing the friends not only to each other, but to Himself:

> Thus ascending from that holy love with which he embraces a friend to that with which he embraces Christ, he will partake joyfully and in abundance of the spiritual fruit of friendship, awaiting the fullness of all things in the life to come.... Then we shall rejoice in the eternal possession of Supreme Goodness, and this friendship to which here we admit but few, will be outpoured upon all and by all outpoured upon God, and God shall be all in all (Aelred, *loc. cit.*, n. 134).

The life of consecrated virginity will keep us open to fraternal intimacy and friendship, both as a *way* to God, as often happens in spiritual direction, and as an *expression* of God's inexhaustible friendship. We do not come to the monastery to seek friends. However, we do *find* them. We discover that a true Christian friendship is ascetically demanding, deeply detached, and emotionally free. Not without reason, many Desert Fathers stress the relation between anger and lust on the one hand, and fraternal meekness and chastity on the other. Brotherly love is meant to be a gauge of chastity, a school of patience and truth:

> Abba Hyperechios said, "He who does not control his tongue when he is angry, will not control his passions either." He also said, "It is better to eat meat and drink wine rather than to eat the flesh of one's brethren through slander."

The close communal nature of cenobitic life usually means that it is not so much the brother's human accidents which are loved—God is loved in him. Even better, God's own love in you sparks your love for the brother who then becomes your friend. You love your companions not so much because they are naturally pleasing as because they are the brothers chosen for you by God and with whom you are intimately united in the mystery of salvation. This implies a deep, sensitive affection, but it is not necessarily sentimental.

A healthy monastic friendship thus tends to express itself in a double spirit of sacrifice and solitude. It is not so much a matter of putting yourself out for this or that "friend" and expecting that he do the same for you, but you express your love for your brother by sacrificing yourself for the community, for *all* the brothers without distinction. The monk does not "need" consolations from his friends. He is glad of their company, but he is also glad to be alone. He knows how to communicate peacefully and to dialogue with clarity of expression, but he also knows how to be alone peacefully, with clarity of heart.

Brotherly love in general, and spiritual friendship in particular, is, then, a kind of meeting place of the different levels of sexuality insofar as they have surrendered themselves to the chastity of Christ. It implies the capacity to live alone in community, closely united to our brothers without excessive need for special recognition or expressions of friendship, yet open to them on the deepest level of our being as co-members of the one Body of Christ. It implies the ability and the desire to affirm them in their own spiritual way, as persons dearly loved by God.

Without openness to brotherly love, there is real danger that this form of human love and sexuality will "go underground" and appear in a multitude of unhealthy and obscure ways, both inside and outside the monastery. This seems to be the message of the Council's reference to the matter:

> Above all, everyone should remember—especially superiors—that chastity has stronger safeguards in a community when true fraternal love thrives among its members.... They should be trained to make a celibate life consecrated to God part of the richness of their personality (PC 12).

In the preceding pages we have touched the main implications of our vow of consecrated virginity. We can sum up here the more important practical points:

-Accept your sexuality with optimism, self-control, and a sense of personal responsibility. God has given it to you as something beautiful and dynamic. It shares to a high degree in His plan to "unite all things, in heaven and on earth, under one head, Christ" (Eph. 1:10).

-The control of your sexuality, which is the task of chastity, can make use of simple physical means, such as productive work, healthy visual symbols, yoga postures, etc., but it is above all a matter of orienting sexual energy to higher forms of self-giving.

-This self-gift can and should be channeled through work and service to the community, but it is especially achieved through healthy interpersonal relations. Look upon your brother in his deepest self, not as though he were something to be used for your personal advantage or gratification.

-Develop brotherly love or spiritual friendship, putting more emphasis on what you give than on what you receive. Loyalty and peace are more important than a somewhat sentimental search for intimacy.

-In relations with the opposite sex, be your true self. Both excessive fear and excessive enthusiasm spring from an immature chastity. If your sexual center of gravity is more mature, based on fraternal love and the love of Christ, then relations with the other sex can help integrate certain aspects of your personality which may otherwise remain dormant.

-In community, avoid manifestations of special affection or special favors for certain brothers and not for others. Do not seek out the company of those for whom you have a special liking. Special affection for some is normal, but its expressions must be controlled, so that such friendships can be a part of divine love and not just a fruit of human possessiveness.

-As soon as any difficulty with chastity, sexuality, or particular affections start interfering with your life of prayer or peace of heart, discuss it in spiritual direction and follow the advice given. The reason for this is not arbitrary, or solely based on the value of humility, though this has a lot to do with the value of self-revelation. Nevertheless, the underlying cause is the network of reciprocal influences among the different levels of your sexuality. A humble revelation of self, of one's problems, needs, desires, and drives constitutes in itself a very efficacious channeling of sexuality into new, healthy dimensions of mature personal relations. Divine love itself, in the Person of the Holy Spirit, enters into such relations and purifies the heart in a way which no merely human method can do.

"To the degree that the faithful understand the excellence and necessity of chastity in the life of men and women, so will they perceive, by a type of spiritual instinct, what chastity demands and counsels. And they will also know better how to accept and fulfill, in docility to the Church's teaching, what a rightly formed conscience tells them in concrete cases" (PH 11).

3. FRUITS OF CONSECRATED VIRGINITY

Greater insight into the nature of human sexuality should produce a more delicate sensitivity to the different inner dimensions of Christian chastity. We have sketched these dimensions in the previous section of this chapter. Special attention, however, must always be given to the Christocentric nature of our vow.

Sponsa Christi

We shall never penetrate sufficiently the nobility and the beauty of consecrated Christian virginity. It is true that married life also has a deep nobility and beauty. It is a vocation worthy of all Christians. It is also true that lack of a normal home life puts our affectivity under a real tension. But the beauty and the human advantages of married life ought to make us appreciate even more, and commit ourselves with even more enthusiasm to, the life of absolute fidelity to the Person of Christ. He is the soul of Christian chastity and its principal fruit.

To be a spouse of Christ! If we could only understand the grandeur, the privilege, and all the sanctifying force of the reality expressed by these words! You belong to the Son of God, not only by desire or intention, but by a consecration of body and soul. And He, in His turn, belongs to you. He gives you the strength, the vision, and the balance necessary to fulfill this vow faithfully and patiently, so that even in this life you can experience the joy and fecundity which He has reserved for those who are truly His in a nuptial union:

> This total continence for the kingdom of heaven has always been held by the Church in the greatest esteem, as a sign and stimulus of charity and as an extraordinary source of spiritual fertility in the world (LG 42).

Here as elsewhere, our model is Mary, the Virgin Mother of the Church.

PRAYER

Spiritual marriage with Christ integrates into itself all other dimensions of human existence: sexuality, intellect, will, imagination, memory, the passions, the spirit. It does this through *love*, divine love restoring human love in Christ. Love seeks the person and the presence of the Beloved. Besides a life of self-denial and besides openness in fraternal charity, which are two expressions of this divine love, there is also necessary, even more necessary, a solitary and personal communion in which the inner heart is alone with the Beloved and surrenders itself to Him in silence and recollection. Prayer is basically an act of love.

From this often obscure experience of God's presence by love comes a desire to praise Him, to declare His great goodness to all men, to give ourselves to Him more completely, to unite ourselves with all our brothers and with all creation in a single act of celebration and sacrifice. This is the heart of liturgy, contemplation, monastic life, and the Church itself.

In practice the key to such nuptial love is *faith*. In fact faith forms a single spiritual force with Christian hope and love. It is the only adequate means at our disposal for union with Christ, and therefore must be the guiding light—or the guiding darkness—throughout the spiritual journey.

This implies, on the one hand, that the love of Christ shines in you as a divine light, as a special creation of God, a personal revelation. Faith is not just your own inner light, the light of conscience, but the inner "mind" of Christ in you, which both elevates your conscience and submits your entire being to God's plan of salvation. It is the inner echo in you of the Incarnation, Death, and Resurrection of the Lord, an act of inner "obedience by which man entrusts his whole self freely to God who reveals Himself" (DV 5). "Faith is the substance of things to be hoped for" (Heb. 11:1), which means that you have now, in your deepest self, the blinding reality of God's love for you, strengthening you in virginity of intellect and spirit.

On the other hand, the life of faith implies that any search for support or security in sensible feelings of love, spiritual concepts, or even seemingly holy desires is not the direct path to seeing the face of the Spouse. Faith will purify by its own spiritual force all these lower levels of our sexuality, so that their necessary preparatory and symbolic elements do not interfere with what is meant to be a truly personal and nuptial encounter with God. It is above all in prayer that this purification takes place, which explains many of the spiritual battles which prayer can involve.

Virginity and Conversion

From what we have seen in this chapter, we can appreciate more adequately the importance of chastity in the life of the vows. Just as conversion of life is the heart of the monastic life, since it guides and directs all the other elements, one can say that consecrated virginity is the very *heart of conversion of life*.

Precisely because consecrated virginity deprives human nature, on the more superficial levels of its sexuality, of basic satisfactions which it longs for, the vow has the power of mobilizing all the interior faculties of man or woman. Virginity permits a man or woman, as it permitted Christ, to be a living sacrament of God's love beyond what his mere sex is capable of expressing. This is why the state of consecrated virginity is objectively a further developed and more Christ-like state than matrimony.

But, as we have seen, the social state of consecrated virginity has to be interiorized through a process which covers a whole lifetime. In this vow, as in the others, one *grows* toward Christ. Asceticism is vital here, and this is where our vow of conversion of life—which is principally an ascetic vow—can be of invaluable help in integrating our sexuality into our spiritual life. This is indicated somewhat negatively by sayings of the Desert, such as: "If you cannot control your anger, you will not be able to control your lust."

More positively, the life of virginity, when well assumed and centered on Christ through faith, self-discipline, humble openness, and prayer, is a spark plug of deeper love. Virginity makes love grow, first in the direction of *universality* (more visibly expressed in the apostolic religious life), but also in a greater *interiority*, the contemplative dimension. Virginity opens up the road of prayer.

The renouncement of the human development received in married life, if this renouncement is carried out correctly, not only orients existing erotic energy, but also produces new energy in the depths of the heart. Thanks to the intrinsic mercy and truth of divine love, there is a new awakening of the human heart, a deeper integration of the spiritual values of which the opposite sex is merely an exterior incarnation, sign, and channel.

For example, a male religious, when faithful to his life of conversion, brings to the surface of his heart and soul the tenderness, mercy, and delicacy which is usually more characteristic of women. These important qualities of love will express themselves both in human relations and in the life of prayer, giving new unity to his Christian experience. The female religious, for her part, will integrate into her feminine personality the more masculine traits of objectivity, justice, and consistency which are also necessary for true love.

And so a life of chastity, far from frustrating human sexuality, can and should fulfill it through conformity to the image of Christ. Just as monastic conversion of life has as its goal the fullness of God's image in the monk, so does consecrated virginity develop and establish deep within him an unsuspectedly beautiful dimension of this image.

Thus the minimum commitment to renounce marriage and abstain from genital stimuli puts the monk in a state of life in which he can dedicate himself freely to the asceticism of the fundamental monastic observances, and to the purity of love which is their purpose. The monk, on perceiving the fruits of this balanced asceticism in his own life, centers all his attention and responsibilities on a docility to the Spirit of Christ. This is the spirit of virginity: "My Lover belongs to me and I to him," "Devote yourselves entirely to the Lord," "Sons of the resurrection," "Prefer nothing to the love of Christ."

As between its starting point and its goal, all the life of the vows unfolds between these two poles of consecrated virginity:

> -consecration of human sexual love
> -perfect love in the Spirit of Christ which has no end nor measure outside itself.

For Further Reflection

1. If the state of consecrated virginity is objectively a further developed and more Christ-like state than marriage, why is religious profession not a sacrament, as matrimony is?

2. What differences exist between the sexual attractions found in animals and human sexuality?

3. In your own personal experience, has the love of Christ made you more sensitive to other kinds of human love? Or has it frustrated their development?

Bibliography

Aelred of Rievaulx. *Spiritual Friendship*, Cistercian Fathers Series 5. Kalamazoo: Cistercian Publications, 1974.
_____. *The Mirror of Charity*. London: Mowbray, 1962.
Baars, C. W. *Born Only Once*. Chicago: Franciscan Herald Press, 1975.
Evoy, J. J. and Christoph, V. F. *Maturity in the Religious Life*. New York: Sheed and Ward, 1964.
Ford, J. M. *A Trilogy on Wisdom and Celibacy*. Notre Dame, Indiana: Univ. of N. D. Press, 1967.
Fourez, G. *A Light Grasp on Life: An Essay on the Evangelical Life and Celibacy*. Denville, New Jersey: Dimension Books, 1972.
Fromm, E. *The Art of Loving*. New York: Harper and Row, 1962.
Goergen, D. *The Sexual Celibate*. New York: Seabury, 1975.
John of the Cross, St. *The Ascent of Mount Carmel*, in *The Collected Works of St. John of the Cross*. Washington: ICS Publication, 1973, esp. pp. 73-87.
_____. *The Dark Night*, ibid., pp. 295-390.
Johnston, W. *Silent Music*, pp. 139-166.
Joyce, M. R. and R. E. *New Dynamics in Sexual Love*. Collegeville, Minnesota: St. John's Univ. Press, 1970.
Legrand, L. *The Biblical Doctrine of Virginity*. New York: Sheed and Ward, 1963.
Lepp, I. *The Psychology of Loving*. Baltimore: Helicon Press, 1963.
_____. *The Ways of Friendship*. New York: Macmillan, 1966.
Lewis, C. S. *The Four Loves*. New York: Harcourt, Brace, 1960.
Louf, A. *Teach us to Pray*, pp. 59-68.
May, R. *Love and Will*. New York: Norton, 1969.
Merton, T. *Mystics and Zen Masters*. New York: Farrar, Straus, 1967, pp. 113-127.
Peifer, C. *Monastic Spirituality*, pp. 258-271.
Raguin, Y. *Celibacy for Our Times*, Religious Experience Series 7. St. Meinrad, Indiana: Abbey Press, 1974.
Rees, D., et al. *Consider Your Call*, pp. 154-188.
Ricoeur, P. *Fallible Man*. Chicago: H. Regnery, 1967.
Stern, K. *The Flight From Woman*. New York: Farrar, Straus, 1969.
Thurian, M. *Marriage and Celibacy*. London: S. C. M. Press, 1959.
Voillaume, R. *Seeds of the Desert*. London: Burns and Oates; Notre Dame: Fides, 1955, pp. 304-334.
Vidal, M. *Moral del amor y de sexualidad*. Salamanca: Sigueme, 1972.

CHAPTER FOUR

POVERTY

Whereas virginity consecrated to Christ constitutes the central and most primitive nucleus of the life of the vows, religious poverty, the public renunciation of the use and possession of material goods, causes this consecration "for the kingdom of heaven" to reach into new dimensions of human existence.

This can be seen in the fact that, from the viewpoint of the Old Testament, and in general of the world that does not know the mystery of Christ, virginity is a radical and almost intolerable poverty. Sexual relations and the bearing of children are glorious expressions of manhood or womanhood, whereas virginity corresponds to sterility. In this line of thought, virginity is a *sign of deep human poverty*, which leads the way to confidence in the spiritual fecundity of the risen Christ.

But from another point of view, insofar as it is a consecration to the kingdom of God, the only enduring kingdom, poverty is an *irradiation of virginity over material things*. Material goods are left behind and, by that very fact, transformed by the light of the resurrection as it shines upon them through human hearts purified of the possessive instinct.

1. TYPES OF RELIGIOUS POVERTY

Because it deals with material goods and their use, the practice of poverty leaves ample room to the particular purpose of each religious institute. *No other vow depends so much on the spirit in which it is practiced*, and therefore with no other vow is it so important to understand the mentality, the necessities, and the particular nature of the religious institute in which one lives. For example, the use of material goods on the part of a religious administrator of a hospital in the center of New York City will be distinct from that practiced by a missionary in charge of a country parish. And both are going to be different from the poverty of a Carthusian in his cell.

The reason for these differences is simply that poverty is a means to something better—perfection in love and in the fulfillment of one's particular vocation. Saint Thomas Aquinas put it this way:

A doctor does not heal his patient inasmuch as he gives him a greater quantity of medicine, but insofar as this medicine is more adequate for the infirmity. Likewise, a religious community will not be better for having greater poverty, but insofar as this poverty is more proportioned to the common end of religious life and to the special mission of the Institute (ST II-II 188, 7 ad 1).

Contemporary writers on the religious life repeatedly point out that external poverty assumes a variety of forms and will differ from one religious institute to another. There are three interacting reasons for this variety: the wide gambit of internal dispositions and graces, the complexity of today's pluralistic culture, and the different tasks that the workers in the kingdom of God must bring to completion in such circumstances. The directives of Vatican II reflect these different factors:

The manner of living, praying, and working should be suitably adapted to the physical and psychological conditions of today's religious and also, to the extent required by the nature of each community, to the needs of the apostolate, the requirements of a given culture, the social and economic circumstances (PC 3).

The emphasis put here on the "nature of each community" leads us to the important question: What is Benedictine or Cistercian poverty?

Benedictine Poverty

Since the practice of religious poverty depends so much on the specific character of our life, and this is expressed in a special way through the Rule of Saint Benedict, let us see the principal places where the Rule speaks of the use of material goods.

DISTRIBUTION OF GOODS:

Let all things be common to all, as it is written, and let no one say or think that anything is his own. And if someone be caught in this most wicked vice, let him be admonished (RB 33).

Let no one dare give or receive anything without permission of the abbot, nor have anything as his own, anything whatever...since they are not permitted to have even their bodies or their wills at their own disposal. But they are to look for all that is necessary from the Father of the monastery (RB 33).

As it is written: distribution was made to each according as he had need. By this we do not mean that there should be respect of persons (God forbid!), but consideration for weaknesses (RB 34).

If anyone be found to have something which he did not receive from the abbot, let him be subjected to the strictest punishment. And in order to cut out this vice of private ownership by the roots, let the abbot provide whatever may be necessary (RB 55).

INTERIOR DISPOSITIONS:

He who needs less should thank God and not be discontented; but he who needs more should be humbled by the thought of his infirmity rather than feeling important on account of the kindness shown him. Thus all the members will be at peace. Above all, let not the evil of murmuring appear for any reason whatsoever in the least word or sign (RB 34).

Let no one be troubled or saddened in the house of God (RB 31).

Let the monk be content with the poorest and worst of everything (RB 7).

ADMINISTRATION:

Let the house of God be wisely administered by wise men (RB 53).

The monastery, as much as possible, ought to be constructed in such a way that all that is necessary...and the different employments may be within the enclosure, so that the monks need not wander outside (RB 66).

He who administers well wins for himself a good standing (RB 31).

If any products of the craftsmen are to be sold, let those who have to manage the business take care that they be not guilty of any dishonesty.... As regards the price, let not the sin of avarice creep in, but let the goods always be sold a little cheaper than they are sold by people of the world, so that in all things God may be glorified (RB 57).

VALUE OF MATERIAL GOODS:

Let him look upon all the utensils of the monastery and its whole property as upon the sacred vessels of the altar. Let him not think that anything may be neglected. Let him neither practice avarice, nor be wasteful and a squanderer of the monastery's substance; but let him do all things with measure and in accordance with the instructions of the abbot (RB 31).

If anyone treats the things of the monastery in a slovenly or careless way, he should be corrected (RB 32).

He who is finishing his week's duties in the kitchen shall return the utensils of his office clean and in good condition to the cellarer. And the cellarer, in his turn, will deliver them to him who is entering, so that he may know what he gives out and what he receives back (RB 35).

Let the abbot confide the goods of the monastery, tools, clothing, and everything else to monks on whose life and character he can rely (RB 32).

DIGNITY OF THE HUMAN PERSON:

> Above all and before all let care be taken of the sick brethren, so that they be served as Christ in person.... Therefore, let the abbot have the greatest care that they suffer no neglect (RB 36).

> To whom he cannot give what was asked, let him give at least a kind word in reply, because it is written: "A good word is worth more than the most precious gift" (RB 31).

> Let the abbot be attentive to the weaknesses of the needy, not to the ill-will of the envious (RB 55).

> Let not the abbot overlook or undervalue the salvation of the souls confided to him, giving more attention to transitory, worldly, and perishable things... and if he be tempted to complain for lack of means let him remember that which is written: "Seek first the kingdom of God and His justice and all these things will be given to you besides" (RB 2).

> In his commands let him be prudent and considerate; and whether the work which he enjoins concerns God or the world, let him be discreet and moderate, bearing in mind the discretion of holy Jacob, who said, "If I cause my flocks to be overdriven, they will all die in one day" (RB 64).

> Let him order all things so that the strong monks desire to do more and the weak ones do not shrink back (RB 64).

We have quoted all these texts from the Rule because, in making our profession and above all in *living it*, we do so "according to the Rule of Saint Benedict." This explains the importance of knowing his approach to the practice of monastic poverty.

Personal Poverty

In the Rule, we can see that the preoccupation of Saint Benedict in speaking of the use of material goods is not that the monastery be as poor as possible, but rather that it be as full as possible of peace, fraternal communion, and the spirit of Christian sacrifice. What matters for Saint Benedict is not primarily the poverty of the monastery as a whole, what could be called "sociological poverty," but rather *ascetical and personal poverty directed toward a spiritual dependence on Christ as represented by the abbot, toward a sense of responsibility for material goods, and toward the true peace of the brethren.*

The task of the abbot is principally to measure the demands of the common life according to the capacities of each brother. From the brethren, Benedict expects a sense of personal responsibility and vigilance, with a complete dependence on the abbot as an efficacious sign of their dependence on Christ.

Communal Poverty

The personal aspect, however, is not the only one foreseen by the Rule. There is a second aspect which is also ascetical and equally directed toward a sense of responsibility and peace—*the community as a whole ought to use its goods in such a way that "in all things God may be glorified."* Saint Benedict describes three concrete applications of this universal principle: generous hospitality toward the poor (RB 53), reduced prices in the sale of the monastery's produce (RB 57), possession of the necessary land and workshops so as to guarantee effective withdrawal from society (RB 66).

This communal aspect receives more attention at the present time, as the Council pointed out:

> Poverty voluntarily embraced in imitation of Christ provides a witness which is highly esteemed, especially today.... Religious poverty requires more than limiting the use of possessions to the consent of superiors; members of a community ought to be poor in both fact and spirit, and have their treasures in heaven (cf. Mt. 6:20).... To the degree that their rules and constitutions permit religious communities can rightly possess whatever is necessary for their temporal life and their mission. Still, let them avoid every appearance of luxury, of excessive wealth, and accumulation of possessions (PC 13).

According to this, it is clear that the monk of today has an important obligation to embrace poverty not only as an individual, but also on a community level.

What does all this imply for the practice of monastic poverty?

2. OUR RESPONSIBILITIES

The commitment of monastic poverty can be reduced to three general responsibilities: personal poverty and detachment, common life and productive work as expressions of personal poverty, and active participation, according to our position in the community, in communal poverty.

Personal Poverty and Detachment

This more interior dimension maintains all its importance. It implies dependence on the superior in the use of material goods prior to final profession and in both using and possessing them after such profession.

This is vital. Often those who criticize the apparent lack of community poverty, the size of the buildings, the extent of the land-holdings, or the use of modern machinery are those who least have a sense of personal poverty. They are anxious to have the best commodities and to work as little as possible. If they are monks, they hoard books, photos, cards, and souvenirs in their private room. They ask for a special diet, special work, special permissions. *Without a strong spirit and profound love of personal poverty, all attempts at communal poverty are pure hypocrisy and can be very dangerous for the monk,* distracting him from the central meaning of his vocation—total detachment from all creatures in order to love Christ with all his heart and love all else in Him and for Him.

Thus the first duty of the monk in the matter of poverty is to live it perfectly in his own life, within the community and in dependence on his superiors. Only thus will he be able to see the true necessities, exigencies, and measures of communal poverty. In our life, an expression of personal poverty is frequently the acceptance of a communitarian poverty which is less austere than what we desire it to be.

One of the keys to religious poverty is the difference between what is *useful* and what is *superfluous*. The superfluous, be it private or collective, has to be banished in virtue of the law of universal fraternal charity, which cannot suffer superfluities when others suffer need. What is useful, on the other hand, can, and many times must be kept.

However, in order to be sensitive to the dividing line between the useful and the superfluous, we need sincere detachment. First personal detachment, in order to suppress all that is superfluous and be increasingly aware of what is not too necessary. Then collective detachment, in order to reduce community needs to a minimum, living in sober austerity with a simple standard of life. A religious community should arrive at the point of renouncing the satisfactions of conveniences and comfort, at least under the aspect of the pleasures which they offer, if not in what they have of real usefulness. We should realize that comfort is the mask with which the wealth and riches of much of our society are disguised. This is true in any country, but it has a special importance when we are living in or related to countries of the Third or Fourth World. The destitute people and poorer classes in these countries often have cultural values which are superior to our own and are very sensitive to the fact that Christianity and wealth have often gone hand in hand. No monastery can escape this problem, and only a deep spirit of personal poverty can recognize the demands of both prudence and sacrifice which such a situation imposes on us all.

This is why effective poverty is never achieved by regulations and pressure tactics. *It is a work of love.* Only love of poverty, or rather love of the poor Christ, can give an objectively balanced judgment concerning what is strictly necessary for our life.

This love expresses itself in a tendency—the monk desires to become more poor. This "poverty of spirit," this love of poverty as an expression of the love of Christ, is the immediate end of the vow of poverty. It is the spirit expressed by Saint Benedict (RB 34, 3-4): "Let him who needs less give thanks to God...let him who needs more be humbled by his weakness." If we really loved, the practice of poverty would cease to be one of those problems which are indefinitely present to our doubting spirit. This love would bring us to what is simple and humble (which does not mean what is ugly), and we would look for everything from our Father in heaven, whose chief interpreter for us is the abbot. We would even know how to refuse many expensive items which benefactors might desire to give us.

Common Life and Productive Work

These are the primary consequences of personal poverty. By his vow of conversion of life, the monk promises to live in common, sharing the lot of his brothers, working to support the community.

In a previous chapter we have seen our responsibilities in regard to these observances. We should realize that the common life is a fundamental expression of poverty and becomes more difficult with the years. The tendency to make a little corner for oneself, perhaps a private office, to appropriate things such as special books, clothes, or typewriters, becomes stronger with time if we do not discipline ourselves from the beginning of the novitiate in a positive and generous practice of detachment from the comforts that our cenobitic life offers us. A good remedy: periodic examinations of conscience, for example, each year during our annual retreat.

Productive work, which includes services such as those of secretary, guestmaster, superior, or librarian, is also a fundamental expression of poverty. We can say that the principal element of monastic poverty is that the monk work to sustain the community. In practice, the monk who is faithful to the common life and to productive work is living his vow of poverty.

THE CISTERCIAN REFORM AND THE PRACTICE OF POVERTY

A look at the spirit of the Cistercian reform can make us more sensitive to the meaning of monastic poverty. The first Cistercians expressed the principles and ideals of their renewal of Benedictine life in the *Exordium Parvum*, a document of some fifteen pages which narrates the story of the first years of Citeaux. In these pages we can see how important a role effective communal poverty played in their reform.

"Poor with the poor Christ," says the *Exordium Parvum* as it describes the founders of Citeaux. Reacting against certain abuses of the Cluniac monasteries, the first Cistercians proclaimed their return to the simplicity of the Rule of Saint Benedict, with special emphasis on the following points:

-*Clothing*—elimination of fine garments, special colors, furs, embroidered hoods.

-*Food*—simplicity of menu, elimination of animal fat.

-*Work*—This is the key to Cistercian poverty. It ought to be productive, and therefore manual work was preferred. Intellectual work (study, writing) was not favored very much, although not condemned. The copying of manuscripts was considered to be manual labor since it was for the use of others and for the community. The primary goal was that the Cistercian monk not depend on the work of others for his support. Therefore parishes, chapels, cemeteries and ecclesiastical benefices, tithes, public mills and bakeries, and the possession of serfs were rejected as sources of income.

Today productive labor continues to have an immense importance not only for personal poverty (we have already seen it as one of the basic observances included in the vow of conversion of life), but also for the poverty of the community. A monastery which is set apart, stable, well organized, mechanized, and having land will hardly ever witness to social poverty as do, for example, the Little Brothers of Jesus according to the spirit of Charles de Foucauld, or the Missionaries of Charity of Mother Teresa of Calcutta. Our vocation is not to give this type of witness and the Church does not expect it from us. Our most authentic witness will be that of the primacy of prayer and contemplation over all the other works of man. It will be the example of Christ praying alone on the mountain, in the desert, in Gethsemane, and on the cross.

But the Church and the world have the right to look to us for the witness of work. The work of a monk has a special dignity, not by what is externally achieved but because it is done by a person completely given to God. It witnesses to the fact that the work of every man only has its true meaning in the light of the resurrection of Christ, and that, on the other hand, *all* human work is worthy of a son of God, thanks to the power of the risen Christ. In practice, fidelity to work, with a generosity and sacrifice of one's interests in its fulfillment, is a guarantee of our fidelity to the demands of monastic poverty, both on the individual level and as a community.

-Simplicity especially in the liturgy—The first Cistercians suppressed the use of precious objects such as embroidered vestments, gold chalices, or costly paintings. Above all, they sought for a simplification of prayer, where the practice of poverty could penetrate even within their life of prayer, reading, or study. In Citeaux, everything was characterized by simplicity and the absence of complicated methods.

Here we touch something very close to the Heart of Christ—*spiritual poverty*. "Happy the poor of heart, because theirs is the kingdom of heaven." This does not signify the mere interior detachment from material goods nor a "spirit" of poverty disembodied from a concrete exterior situation. *Spiritual poverty is this absence of complicated methods, both exterior* (conveniences, dominion over things and persons, excessive refinement) *and interior* (a spirituality based on our own efforts, our own virtues, exotic methods of prayer, formalisms, or excessive introspection).

It is the exterior and interior simplicity of life led by the faithful poor of the Old and New Testaments, the *Anawim*: fidelity to God amid the absence of luxury; a spirit of abandonment, joy, and brotherhood; above all, *humility*. The Virgin Mary and Jesus Himself are the great "poor ones of the Lord," completely docile to the will of the Heavenly Father. This spirit is summed up and promulgated in the words of the Lord: "Learn of me, that I am gentle and humble of heart, and you will find rest for your souls" (Mt. 11:29).

Thus this spiritual poverty is very close to the purity of heart, perfect humility, and love which constitute the purpose of all the monastic observances and, indeed, of all Christian spirituality.

-Solitude—This is another important aspect of Cistercian poverty underlined by the *Exordium Parvum*. It eliminates as much as possible contacts with the world, business trips, and the reception of the nobility within the enclosure. Nowadays this element of our poverty is also made palpable by the limited information that we receive—the relative

lack of newspapers, radio, T.V., or movies. The fact that this separation attracts and pleases us does not lessen the force of solitude as an expression of poverty and abandonment to God. Poverty is not always that which is most difficult.

Historically, the importance of poverty, work, and solitude gave rise to the institution of the Lay Brothers, who directed the greater part of the work of Benedictine and Cistercian monasteries until the 1960s. "Familiars" also worked as members of the monastic family. In our days, new factors play an important part in the practice of work and poverty within the monastic life. For example, there is a greatly increased dependence on external factors such as the purchase of machines with their special parts, and, in general, the more complicated aspects of contemporary economic life ("socialization"). The repercussions of economic factors on moral issues such as war and peace, development of the poorer nations, or unjust social structures in general, are also important.

We should take these modern realities into account in judging the practice of monastic poverty in our days. It is also necessary to be familiar with the social doctrine of the Church, especially with the different possible applications of its fundamental principle—the universal destination of earthly goods (GS 69). The integration of the Lay Brothers into the community, with only one class of monks, is simply one example of how we should seek new ways of expressing monastic poverty which will not be completely the same as those of past centuries.

Responsibility for the Community's Collective Poverty

This third general expression of monastic poverty is relatively new. Vatican II (PC 13) has indicated to us with a gentle but firm hand that each religious ought to feel responsible not only for his own personal poverty, his personal dependence on superiors in the use of the goods of the monastery, and his own personal generosity in the common life or at work, but also for the poverty of the community as a whole.

Actually, Saint Benedict foresaw this coresponsibility in his chapter on calling the brothers to counsel:

> As often as any important business has to be done in the monastery, let the abbot call together the whole community and himself set forth the matter.... The reason why we have said that all should be called to counsel is that the Lord often reveals to a younger brother what is best. So the brothers should give their advice with all deference and humility, and not presume stubbornly to defend their opinions (RB 3, 1-4).

Now "poverty voluntarily embraced in imitation of Christ provides a witness which is highly esteemed, especially nowadays" (PC 13). Therefore, the determination of the concrete expressions of a community's monastic poverty is not only the task of the superiors, but of all the brothers, *each one according to his position in the community.*

It would be a mistake to think that the monk ought not to concern himself with such practical, material, and at times, complicated affairs, or that his entrance into the community has freed him of all that. This would be a false idealism.

It is true that at the beginning of his "conversion," during the first years of his formation, the novice and the young monk have much more important and more personal things to do. The practice and the spirit of *personal* poverty must come before that of collective poverty. A period of freedom from material responsibilities is necessary to sound the depths of the mystery of Christ.

But this very mystery of Christ is going to impel the monk to become aware of his place, his function, and his responsibilities in the Pilgrim Church and within humanity as a whole. *Before the time of his final profession, the monk should be able to take an active part in the material interests of the community and to make an intelligent judgment on the communitarian practice of poverty.*

What are the factors that we should take into account in forming such a judgment?

There are three principal criteria:

-*The standard of living of the poorer families who live near the monastery.* Poverty is something real and concrete, and its foundation cannot be less real and concrete. The community ought to consider itself and be considered by others as a community of poor people, united in Christ. Nevertheless, this norm must be complemented by the two following factors:

-*The contemplative nature of our life.* Monastic poverty should aid us to reach our ideal of contemplative union with God. In other words, poverty is for the monk and not the monk for poverty. If the lack of goods and resources came to be a continual distraction and preoccupation, it would be a harmful perversion of authentic monastic poverty.

Thus it is normal that we spend less than many families for our food and clothing, but much more than they in books, in buildings, and for heating the places where our manner of life obliges us to remain for long periods without moving around.

Concerning buildings in general, it can be said that our houses, though of modest proportions, ought to express a certain harmony of form. Luxury is one thing, but beauty is another. According as the enclosure and the rule are more strict, so much more does mental hygiene indicate that the exterior and interior environment should permit a certain expansion of our affective faculties in their search for what is beautiful.

   -*The physical, psychological, and moral abilities of the members of our community.*

A saying of the Fathers of the Desert illustrates this third criterion:

One day Abba Mark said to Abba Arsenius, "It is very good, isn't it, not to have anything in your cell that would be solely to satisfy a personal whim? For example, I once knew a brother who had a little wild flower which sprang up from the earth in his cell. He pulled it up by the roots." Abba Arsenius answered, "That is all right. But each person should act according to his own spiritual way. And if the brother cannot live without the flower, he ought to plant it again."

In the same sense, Saint Benedict insists that the abbot always take into account the weaknesses of the brothers and that "he order all things in such a way that the strong desire more and the weak be not discouraged" (RB 64, 19).

If the nature of cenobitic poverty requires that we all share in the responsibility of the abbot for the poverty of the monastery, we must also participate in his responsibility for the souls confided to him. We shall have to accept the fact that the cenobitic life will always be much less "poor" in the material sense than the life of a hermit, due to the multiplication of personal needs.

To take into account and accept human limitations is part of the discretion required by the life of the vows in general and by poverty in particular. True humility and interior poverty will know how to live poorly in a monastery which is less poor than the ideal monastic setting.

3. TOWARD A MATURE POVERTY

Poverty is something that unfolds. Like the other vows, it is a talent which God has given you so that you may work with it and gain thirty-, sixty-, and a hundredfold. Poverty must *grow*. Your baptismal grace is ordered to this growth. The vow of conversion of life reinforces this obligation and creates excellent conditions for its fulfillment.

Immature Poverty

Many monks believe that the vow of poverty is well observed if they have everything with permission. They never grow in poverty, but simply "observe" poverty. And by satisfying, always with permission, their desires to acquire more things, they lose little by little that spirit of sacrifice which constitutes the very soul of monastic life. They never really accept the fact that poverty consists in *not having what they want*.

The great reality is that Jesus wants to be all our joy. But He will not be able to achieve this if we are tied down to anything. Therefore, having fulfilled the responsibilities that we have seen above, there remains an extensive area in which to grow in the life of poverty. Not until we renounce for love of Jesus the good things and the human values that have contributed to our material well-being do we prove that we prefer Him to all else, and that only from Him do we expect to receive all our joy. Really, the mere fact of not offending God is hardly enough to enable us to say that we are faithful in His service. True love is much more demanding.

Growth in the Life of Poverty

As the monk grows in the spirit of conversion of life, he *restricts his necessities*. He learns to live with less. Obviously, monastic poverty does not mean eliminating the necessary things of life—food, clothing, shelter, tools. Nevertheless, the monk becomes increasingly aware that some things are superfluous, that what was necessary before is not so vital in reality and that he can live without it. He grows in the desire for sacrifice. He wants to have less. He seeks opportunities to sacrifice himself, especially when such sacrifice can benefit others.

The good of poverty is found precisely in the fact that it despoils us, frees us, makes us sensitive to the needs of others, and opens our eyes which have been blinded by superficial and transitory sense goods. It thus permits us to acquire true goods, which are those of inner generosity, sharing, and the gift of self. It opens the doors for us to the secret joy of Christ's patient, gentle, and humble heart.

Saint Basil, in his *Long Rules* (Question 8), writes that the monk "will deem all possessions foreign to him, as indeed they are." He does not deny that the riches of the world (money, fame, prestige, success, eloquence) are goods, but he affirms that these goods are "foreign" to the monk. Why? Because the monk is a "citizen of heaven" (Phil. 3:20). He belongs to a new world. His goods are the goods of the kingdom made present in Jesus Christ. His wealth is God Himself. All the rest is "foreign" to him. He is happy to give it away.

The spirit of sacrifice of all that is not God can enter into many aspects of the life of the monk—not only his personal objects, which might be useful, but also his time, his likes and dislikes, his work, even the inclinations of his temperament and his spiritual desires. He lets himself be emptied:

-*Exterior poverty* is essential before you can advance into the realm of real interior poverty. Do not kid yourself that you are practicing poverty of spirit if exteriorly you are accumulating useless objects and permissions, and protecting yourself against the hardships of life by all kinds of shock absorbers. This is not poverty or freedom, it is only weakness and evasion.

-*Interior poverty*, based on serious exterior poverty, is an emptying of self and an inner deprivation, a death of self, a disappearance of "I" and "Mine." One ceases to be attached to one's desires, opinions, tastes, virtues, spirituality, progress, everything that makes the "I" solid and evident even in apparently good things. It is better for the "I" to disappear. One should desire to lose this "I," this "self" for the sake of Christ. Thus to lose oneself is to find oneself, and thus to die is to be saved, to live in Christ. This should be our ideal. Without such an ideal, our monastic life will not be solid. And we cannot really be happy in the monastery.

For Further Reflection

1. Do you think that religious poverty is more important for us now than it was for the monks at the time of Saint Benedict or at the moment of the Cistercian reform? Why?

2. Is it correct to say that Saint Benedict is more concerned with "disappropriation"—having nothing of one's own—than with poverty? Does this describe his purpose accurately? Is it sufficient for the monk or nun of today?

3. Are you satisfied with your own personal life of religious poverty? With that of your community?

Bibliography

CLAR (Confederation of Latin American Religious). *Pobreza y Vida Religiosa en America Latina.* Bogota: CLAR, 1970.
Colorado, A. *Los Consejos Evangelicos a la luz de la teologia actual.* Salamanca: Sigueme, 1965, pp. 186-245.

Exordium Parvum, Critical Latin text in J. Bouton and J. Van Damme, *Les plus anciens textes de Citeaux*. Achel, Belgium: Abbaye Cistercienne, 1974, pp. 54-86. English translation in L. Lekai (see below), Appendix I.

Lackner, B. *Eleventh-Century Background of Citeaux*, CS 8, 1972, pp. 131-276.

Lekai, L. *The Cistercians*. Kent, Ohio: The Kent State Univ. Press, 1977, esp. chapters 1-3 and 20-21.

Peifer, C. *Monastic Spirituality*, pp. 247-257.

Rahner, K. "Theology of Poverty" in *Theological Investigations*. Baltimore: Helicon Press; London: Darton, Longman and Todd, 1971, VIII, pp. 168 ff.

Rees, D., et al. *Consider Your Call*, pp. 205-220.

Sortais, G. *Les choses qui plaisent a Dieu*. Begrolles: Abbaye de Bellefontaine, 1967, pp. 71-120.

Voillaume, R. *Seeds of the Desert*, pp. 253-303.

CHAPTER FIVE

MONASTIC OBEDIENCE

1. CHRISTIAN OBEDIENCE

Every person has been created in order to accomplish God's plan in his regard. This implies the need and the inner obligation to obey both God and those who have a right to command, i.e., those who have authority, insofar as this authority, this power to command, comes from God. Thus children obey their parents because the authority of the parents comes to them from God by the very nature of paternity. Married partners have a certain authority over each other's body, with the consequent necessity of obedience. Citizens also owe obedience to the legitimate government of their country; Catholics owe it to their bishop and to the Pope.

Such acts of obedience consist in doing what another person decides should be done, because he has authority, that is, the right to command. This authority over our will must come, at least in an indirect way, from God. Only He can give a right over something so personal and of so much dignity as the human act.

Now *the exercise of authority and the nature of obedience depend on the end of the society in which they are exercised.* Therefore, when authority and obedience are practiced within the Church (for example, between Christian spouses, between priests and bishops, between a monk and his abbot), an intimate relation to the mystery of Christ is added to human obedience in general. By the power of the Holy Spirit which they receive in Baptism and Confirmation, Christians exercise an obedience which is not merely sociological, but also truly charismatic, that is, spiritual, according to the grace and the mission which each one has received from the Lord. This specifically Christian obedience participates in the obedience of Christ to the Father, with all the communion and filial joy that this implies, and also with all the sorrow and suffering that obedience implied for Christ (cf. Heb. 5:8).

The Christian has thus entered explicitly and publicly into the mystery of the redemption of the human race. And this mystery of liberation is common to all—those who command and those who obey. All exercise of obedience and authority in the Church has for its sole purpose our entrance into the salvific will of the Father and our obedience to the Spirit of Christ.

So we can see that Christian obedience is radically distinct from the obedience of a pagan soldier. And the authority of an ecclesiastical superior is very different from that of a policeman. The nature of the Church as "a people made one with the unity of the Father, the Son, and the Holy Spirit..., a community of faith, hope, and charity" (LG 4 and 8), established and continually kept in existence by Christ, the sole mediator, gives to ecclesial authority and obedience a strong mark of *common service to Christ*, Head and Shepherd of His Church, and of *redemptive fellowship with God and with the brethren in Christ*.

2. THE VOW OF OBEDIENCE

What does the vow add to this Christian obedience?

It adds a most efficacious means of entering with more confidence, liberty, and firmness into the mystery of the saving will of the Father. By the vow we place ourselves in the most favorable possible situation for the spirit of obedience and service to increase in us, knowing that this is the way chosen by Christ for bringing the world to its true destiny. The vow implies a totality of availability to this divine process, which other forms of Christian obedience do not.

> Through the profession of obedience, religious offer to God a total dedication of their own wills as a sacrifice of themselves; they thereby unite themselves with greater steadiness and security to the saving will of God.... Thus did Christ Himself out of submission to the Father minister to the brethren and surrender His life as a ransom for many (PC 14).

In this life of service there are two complementary realities which come together and make up the formal objective reason of our obedience: the *community of brothers* united in their common search for the face of Christ, and *Church authority* which approves of and protects the life of the brotherhood. A monastic community is subject to the demands of any human society and thus needs a visible head or guide to be a sign and an instrument of the spiritual thrust shared by the brothers. We accept the authority of this guide when we commit ourselves to the search for God in a specific community. The hierarchy of the Church, for its part, approves our choice and confers on the local superior a participation in its own mission of teaching men to carry out everything that Jesus has commanded (cf. Mt. 28:20). In this way monastic obedience becomes obedience to the Church and in the Church, and we enter deeply into the Father's plan of salvation.

This shows *the importance of a living faith*. God's plan of redemption completely surpasses human intelligence and even goes beyond the supernatural prudence of men, well-intentioned as they may be. Every man is a partially blind instrument of the impenetrable designs of God. But God has established an objective authority, the Church with its ministers of unity and redemption, saying that by means of this visible structure He is going to achieve His saving plan, communicating to all men His grace and His truth. This objective principle enters into the heart and soul of the religious family. All of LG 8 is extremely important as a description of the foundations of our obedience: the community of faith, the society furnished with hierarchical agencies, the imitation of Christ, the apostolic communion, humility, service and poverty, the mystery of sin and the final triumph over it.

Obviously, obedience does not reject human prudence. In fact it uses it all the time. But it rejects it as the ultimate criterion for knowing or fulfilling the saving will of God. Guided by the light of Christian revelation, religious obedience embraces with a total gift of self this ultimate criterion of the loving will of God—the hierarchical communion of the new people of God. *The formal reason for obedience and the direct object of our vow is the divine will, in the discernment of which the authority blessed by God as an expression and an instrument of fellowship in Christ plays the supreme role.* We obey not because it is humanly more secure, but because we enter thus into the great current of grace and truth that flows from God and returns to Him bearing all creation with it.

The vow of obedience, lived in this vision of faith, purifies us from our own point of view, frees us of much human narrowness, and lets us enter into the views and ways of God, which surpass us. Obedience is Jesus who enters our life, who asks and demands our gift of self by means of the persons who cross our path. These persons are men like ourselves. This frequently is hard for our human nature, but the Gospel has never been proposed to us as a comfortable way of life. It leads us to the Father by way of the cross.

3. OBEDIENCE AND CONVERSION OF LIFE

The ways of God are different for each person, according to the vocation which God Himself has given. Each Christian has his own charism. Therefore there exist as many types and modalities in the practice of the vow of obedience as there are institutes of religious life which profess it. It is important to know the *manner* of practicing obedience which is proper to the monastic life, that is to say, the relation between the practice of obedience and conversion of life.

Exterior Commitment

Juridically and exteriorly, the obligations of the vow of obedience extend to the points indicated in many books on religious vows. We should be familiar with these fundamental obligations.

In juridical terms, the motive of our obedience is the dominative power that the superior has over us. How did the superior receive this power? We have seen that inasmuch as he is superior of a community of faith, hope, and love, officially recognized as such, he receives his power from the authority of the Church. But to be *our* superior, he receives his power over us from *us ourselves*. On entering the monastery and on making profession we give ourselves freely to his authority. The Church cannot do this in our place. It is our own commitment. We obey because we want to obey.

This inner freedom of monastic life implies that everyone, superiors and non-superiors, place special emphasis on the ascetic and interior value of obedience, as an expression of faith, inner humility, and communion in the love of Christ. It is interesting to read the Rule, especially Chapters 3, 5, 7, 68, 71, and 72, noting all the times that Saint Benedict underlines the *interior dispositions* of him who obeys. Since monastic life is a life of "conversion," these dispositions enter into the very essence of monastic obedience. For the same reason, the spiritual direction of the abbot or superior, his desires and counsels, have special importance in our life, as does our own personal openness and manifestation of conscience to him or to any spiritual director. The official hierarchical factor is certainly important, especially in situations of doubt or conflict, due to "the superior's authority to decide what be done and to require the doing of it" (PC 14; cf. RB 71, 3). However, our inner dispositions are even more paramount, as is stated in RB 5, 14-18: "The brother must obey willingly since God loves a cheerful giver."

The nature of monastic life also places limits on what a superior can command. He would not be able to command something obviously contrary to conversion of life, for example, sin. He has no right to command a prolonged absence for an end contrary to the nature of the Order, for example, to be a military chaplain or go somewhere for two years solely in order to make money or to help in a parish. A monk who receives an order of this type ought to try gently to dissuade the superior. If the superior insists, the monk should obey for the moment with faith in the impenetrable designs of God, but he has the duty to present the case to the higher superiors.

In the details of monastic living, for the community as a whole and above all for each brother in particular, the abbot or superior has full right, and many times the duty, to adapt and modify things according to the needs and capacities of the brethren. To ask for and to accept permissions and dispensations can be an expression of obedience when there is sufficient reason to do so.

The Holy See, in the name of the Pope, can command that monks do some apostolic work, for example, to be a bishop or a chaplain; the needs of the universal Church prevail in this case over the local needs of the monastic community. This is a result of the fact that we promise obedience, before all others, to the Pope, who is our first superior. Nevertheless, there is little probability that such a demand will ever be made, because the Church has a keen awareness of the apostolic value of institutes dedicated to the contemplative life. See AG 18 and 40; PC 7 and 9; GS 38; VS 1-5.

Spirit of Monastic Obedience

Conversion of life gives a twofold spirit to monastic obedience. It provides its basic orientation: purity of heart and transformation in Christ. It also gives it a specific, though flexible, life setting: the basic Benedictine-Cistercian observances. In this section we shall consider the first of these two relations. The following section deals with the second one, the interdependence of observances and obedience.

The meaning of the monk's obedience is deeply spiritual—the interior transformation worked by complete dedication to the will of Christ. Of course, you can have secondary reasons to obey, such as the economic support of the community, assistance given to others, or the unity of the community, but such reasons, which assume an outstanding role in a religious congregation dedicated to the active apostolate, in our life cede their importance to the principal demand of conversion of heart.

This orientation of obedience is seen in the following saying of the Fathers:

> Abba Hyperechios said: The office of a monk is to obey. If he fulfills it, all that he asks in prayer will be granted to him, and he will stand with confidence before Christ crucified, because the Lord Himself arrived thus to His Cross, made obedient unto death.

The monk obeys in order to unite himself with Christ. The task commanded is secondary. He does not obey for reasons of the apostolate or in order that things turn out well on the human level. In our life there is much less need to judge the order or request in regard to its practical prudence. One obeys *in order to serve* and in order to enter thus into the plan of salvation. Once united to this divine plan, prayer springs forth spontaneously, "in spirit and in truth," and God will fulfill our desires.

Saint Benedict exposes this relation between obedience and conversion with great theological insight: "That you may return by the labor of obedience to Him from whom you have departed by the sloth of disobedience" (RB Prol., 2). These words form part of the first sentence of the Prologue and can be considered as the cornerstone on which the whole Rule is built.

The heart of original sin is *the propensity to do our own will contrary to the will of God*, the tendency to follow our own desires of the moment even when they bring us to the greatest evil. It is the inclination to judge as good that which attracts our self-love. But the way of conversion, the way of holiness, is the way of renunciation of self in order to love God more than ourselves, in order to love not merely the small good of a satisfaction of our own desires, but the great good, the universal and perfect good desired by God. In this universal good we find not merely satisfaction, but eternal peace and happiness through our union with the perfect good which is the loving design of God.

Thus Saint Benedict clearly says there is no love of Christ without the foundation of obedience by which we renounce our attachments and egotism in order *to work with others*:

> An obedience without delay...is the mark of those who hold nothing dearer than Christ (RB 5).

> The brethren ought to obey one another in the assurance that by this path of obedience they will go to God (RB 71).

We have already seen that the vow of conversion of life is the vow to live as a true monk, renouncing the world and cultivating a perfect docility to the voice of Christ. But renouncing the world is not only a question of physically leaving the world and living a manner of life distinct from that of the laity, giving oneself to asceticism and prayer so that God may be glorified in all things. All this is no more than an instrument and a sign of something more central and more important— *the renouncement of self-will*. Only he who renounces his own will in order to collaborate with others in the kingdom of God can survive in the battle against vices, evil thoughts, and fleeting human daydreams. The dynamism of conversion of life leads directly to this battle.

According to RB 71, the monk obeys not only the superiors, but everyone. This obedience to all the brothers, the little acts of service and charity, work, the unperceived renunciation, *everything* has been already consecrated in baptism and is now offered to God by the vow of obedience. Such collaboration with others is the logical consequence of the spiritual childhood preached by Jesus:

> I assure you that if you do not become like little children, you will not enter the kingdom of heaven. Whoever makes himself little like this little child will be the greatest in the kingdom of heaven (Mt. 18:3-4).

It is not by exterior power but by the gentleness of a child at the service of everyone that you enter into the kingdom of the Father. This is the *paschal mystery*—the plan of God demands that you humble yourself before others in order to triumph with Jesus and so enter with Him into the kingdom of the Father. This is the real charism of obedience, which goes beyond and underneath a more sociological and humanly justifiable approach, in order to know Christ from within His own spiritual experience.

This inner spirit of obedience is expressed, for example, in the docility which we give to the advice of a spiritual father, whether he be our canonical superior or not. In this case and in analogous cases of obedience in a broad sense, the deciding factor *for us* is not in the first place the approval by higher authorities, not even the personal qualities of the spiritual director, but rather our own desire, born of grace, to follow Jesus. At first, the spiritual quality of the advice we receive plays the major role in our obedience. But with experience and growth in faith, and often with deep personal struggle, the *inner movement of the spirit which seeks to follow Jesus in His road of self-emptying* comes to predominate. This is one of the key components of the monastic grace. It is the necessary subjective grace which corresponds to the formal objective reason of our obedience, which we saw in the first pages of this chapter.

Reciprocal Need

The vow of obedience "according to the Rule of Saint Benedict," thus finds its spirit within conversion of life. But on the other hand, the promise of conversion is not brought to completion without obedience. They are mutually necessary.

The relation between obedience and conversion is like that which exists between the work of the farmer and the forces of nature. The farmer's work presupposes certain qualities of nature (rain and sun, soil fertility, seed germination rate) and consists principally in making use of all these natural forces in order to have the best possible harvest. But however good the forces of nature may be, if the farmer does not work, if he does not plow, plant, or harvest at the right times, the land will yield little more than thistles and rocks.

Thus it is with the monastic observances and obedience. You can have a desire to attain "perfection," you can keep the obligations of chastity and poverty (up to a certain point), and be faithful enough to the community exercises, but without the work and humiliation of obeying a man the result of the observances will be only the satisfaction of self-love, hypocrisy, and a spirit of criticism.

Another comparison: a monk without the spirit of obedience is like a rider without a horse. He has all that is necessary except what is most essential. The rider cannot function as such without his horse and the monk cannot serve God without obeying. It is the act most typical of the monk. It is that which everyone expects from him. *Obedience is the professional virtue of the monk.* But, on the other hand, the horse without its rider is almost useless. How will he know where to go? Within a short time he will become wild. Thus, too, obedience will lose its meaning and orientation without the spirit of conversion as crystallized in the monastic observances. What is the use of obedience if it is not to deepen conversion of life?

Thus obedience cannot destroy the basic observances of the monastic state, and there are limits as to what the superior can command. This is the sense of the phrase in the formula of profession which we shall study more completely in a later chapter: "according to the Rule of Saint Benedict." Obedience, which is fundamentally a communion in coresponsibility with authority, assumes, personalizes, and brings to fruition the other spiritual methods used in monastic life, just as the labor of the worker assumes, applies, and brings to fruition the forces of nature. Obedience is at the service of conversion of life.

The Word of Christ

Saint Bernard has used another comparison, relating the monastic observances to the six water jugs of the wedding at Cana, in his short sermons, *De Diversis*, 55 and 56. It is worthwhile reading these two brief sermons. You can see in them the close relation between the monastic observances and the perfection of the love of God.

> We understand that the six water jugs placed there symbolize the six observances proposed to the servants of God, in which, like the Jews, they must purify themselves. These are: silence, psalmody, vigils, fasting, manual labor, and purity.... They are full of water when they are observed for fear of God.... They are full of wine when fear is converted into love, when charity excludes fear, when those things that were first observed for fear of punishment are later exercised for the delight and love of justice.... Notice that the water is changed into wine only when the jugs have been filled to overflowing.

Following this comparison, it is precisely *by obedience to the word of Christ* that the servants fill the water jugs, symbols of monastic discipline. It will be for us also the word of Christ, spoken by him who holds His place or by any one of our brothers, especially a spiritual director, which puts the ascetical methods into action, in order to free us from the fear of submission, failure, or inferiority and fill us with the new wine of the love of God.

In passing, it is worth noticing that this application of the miracle of Cana is not only an accommodation of its true meaning, but *is* its true meaning applied to the monastic life. For Saint John, the six water jugs represent the Old Law of the Jews, written on stone and as tasteless as water. The wine is a sign of the Gospel, the New Law of Love, the Holy Spirit, poured out by God in these last times. The conversion of water into wine symbolizes the interior conversion of each Christian from a merely exterior and cold observance to a total docility to the Holy Spirit, the personal Love of God. This continual conversion corresponds exactly to the dynamism of our vow of conversion (See Diagrams I, II, and III in Chapters Two, Seven, and Eight).

Obedience and conversion are mutually necessary. Fidelity to the monastic observances offers the matter on which obedience can work its purifying and transforming effect. And the word of the superior or brother cannot have for its purpose the destruction or contradiction of the observances, but rather their fulfillment and completion by means of something much more dynamic than the observances themselves— the saving will of Christ.

4. DEFECTIVE OBEDIENCE

Besides giving a special spirit to the monk's obedience, our vow of conversion of life demands a more perfect obedience. This is so because Christianity is not a religion of duties and precepts. It is a religion of love (*agape*), the new love which Christ brought to the world with Him, His own love, the love of the Father for the Son and of the Son for the Father, which They desire to be rooted in our hearts. We have seen the implications of this for the practice of Christian chastity. The qualities of our obedience must also be seen in the light of this new love, which is the spirit of conversion.

Sins of Disobedience

A sin, as different from an ethical misbehavior, is a rejection of communion with God. To sin is to refuse to love God and neighbor. By *formal disobedience* we reject the hierarchical communion established by Christ and accepted by us as a means of fulfilling the Father's saving, loving will.

Who are the superiors who represent this hierarchical communion for us?

-The Holy Father, as "successor of Peter, Vicar of Christ, and visible head of the whole Church" (LG 18)

-The Sacred Congregation of Religious, as representing the Holy Father

-The General Chapter, and the Father General or Abbot President, in special cases when the General Chapter is not in session

-The local abbot, and the Father Visitor during the Regular Visitation, when treating the points of the Visitation or when there is no local superior

-The local superior, as delegate of the abbot, in a house which is not autonomous

-The local bishop, in special circumstances in which the house is under his jurisdiction, as happens more often in the case of nuns, although in practice he cedes the exercise of this authority to the Order or Congregation

Not to comply with the explicit and formal commands of these superiors would go against the vow of obedience. In an important matter it would be a serious infidelity.

As we have already seen, the other superiors (Subprior, Cellarer, Father Master, department heads) and even any brother who asks something of us—especially a spiritual director acting as such—also represent this communion with the mystery of Christ. *An habitual negligence*, laziness, carelessness, tardiness at work, for the Divine Office, or in the different employments, usually reveals an infidelity against obedience, according to the degree of voluntary neglect. *He who makes no effort to correct himself*, even in little things, offends against his commitment to obedience.

This negligence can be indirect. That is to say, if I let myself be blinded by a disordered attachment in such a way that I do not recognize the will of the superior or of my brother, I am guilty of disobedience, although at the moment I may not have adverted to the fact of not complying with his command or request. It is enough to know beforehand that preoccupation with my own desires and plans tends to make me careless of the good of the community or the will of the superior. Therefore it is not a completely valid excuse to say, "I didn't realize what you wanted."

We can also fail against obedience by trying to *avoid obeying*: not speaking to the superior when we believe that he wants something that we don't like, not coming to the distribution of work precisely in order to escape a disagreeable request, creating our own jobs in order not to have to work where our presence is really necessary.

Infidelities of this type are directly against the Christian *virtue* or grace of obedience. But they also offend against the *vow* since, *for the person involved*, the vow and the virtue are inseparable, as our initial analysis of the vow has shown. The religious vow does not add anything intrinsic to the Christian virtue, but renders it a great external service by fostering optimum conditions for its growth. When these external conditions are neglected or misused, both vow and virtue suffer. Something very similar happens with the other vows.

Defects in the Spirit of Obedience

An obvious defect is murmuring, a spirit of criticism and habitual resistence to the desires of others. Interiorly, this spirit is directly opposed to the virtue of obedience. If it is carried over to exterior expression it can offend directly against the vow. There is also a real risk of scandal. Complaining is often done without reflection, but there is always danger of scandal.

Other defects would be to cultivate an antipathy or a lack of respect for a superior, to try to escape disagreeable responsibilities as much as possible, to manipulate the superior, to extract permissions by means of sweet words and much persuasion, to menace the superior by means of our emotional reactions (implicitly we say: "I will never be friendly or cooperative with you if you correct me again," or "You will not be able to ask anything of me in the future if you do not give me what I want now"), to obey for very human motives, such as human respect, ambition, vanity, or simply to obey in order to be praised, and not to obey when it will pass unnoticed by men. All this is more or less serious, even though it would be difficult to establish the degree of personal culpability involved.

Religious profession imposes on us a strong obligation to resist and correct these bad dispositions and to examine our conscience concerning our fulfillment of the vow of obedience. Retreat days and the annual retreat are precisely to help us in this. We should not let these times of grace pass by.

How Do We Grow in Obedience?

Here are some suggestions:

-Before all else, *embrace obedience as a work*. We return to God "by the labor of obedience," according to the Prologue of the Rule. It is hard, arduous, and demands sacrifice. At times it is made more difficult with the passing years. If many religious do not grow in obedience it is because they fall into a routine. They presuppose that they are obedient when in reality they have never submitted themselves one hundred percent, body and soul, to the superior. With our modern spirit of independence, obedience can never be taken as a matter of course.

-*Cultivate the life of faith*. This is the most important factor. Our obedience cannot develop without the spirit of faith. As you grow in faith, you grow in obedience and vice versa. He who is not faithful in obedience runs the risk of gradually losing his faith. The cornerstone of monastic obedience is the conviction that what the superior decides is what God wants at the present moment. "*He who hears you, hears Me*" (Lk. 10:16; RB 5, 6 and 15). This in no way should eliminate dialogue, but indicates the necessary inner spirit of both obedience and dialogue.

We have to cultivate these convictions of faith by reading and meditating on the Mystery of the Church, the hierarchic communion as the sacrament of communion with God. Let us think of the obedience of Jesus. Let us ardently *pray* for the grace to grow in obedience. At first we obey Jesus as He speaks to us through others. Then we discover that it is He who obeys in us, and we with Him. Let us have great desires to grow in this way and obey with perfection. God wills it. It is the necessary condition for breaking through the hard crust of our own self-will in order to touch the fertile ground of our deepest self in its openness to God. Just so did Christ "become obedient for us unto death, even unto the death of the cross. For this reason God exalted him" (Phil. 2:8-9).

-*Place the emphasis on humility*. Recognize the fact that disobedience always comes from pride, and that pride is the sin of Satan: "I will not serve. Better to be my own master in hell than to serve in heaven." In reality, this is the complete perversion of liberty. Hell is the incarnation of slavery, interior frustration, and degradation. Fear the spirit of criticism and contradiction. Christ Himself chose the last place and told us to do the same (Lk. 14:10).

-*Submit* everything to the superior, to the Father Master, or to the confessor, until you know what you ought to do.

-Try to enter into the mind of the superior. Be attentive to the desires, which at times are not fully expressed, of others, especially of the superiors.

-Docility and flexibility in everything. Obedience makes you open, pure of heart. Disobedient monks are often stupid and imprudent.

-Cultivate promptness and zeal in obedience. Try to do everything with enthusiasm and intelligence, especially when the task brings with it many difficulties. This is very important in order to prepare us for the exterior and interior purifications that God is going to use in our sanctification. These purifications and difficulties can come from many sides and without warning. We have to be ready and *animated with the love of Christ*, in close union with the dispositions of His Heart, as Saint Paul describes in Phil. 2:5-15.

5. DIALOGUED OBEDIENCE

We have seen during all this analysis of monastic obedience that the motive for uniting yourself to the will of authority—be it the superior or one of the other brothers—is that you thus unite yourself to the divine plan for the salvation of the world. Obedience is our "way to God," as Saint Benedict says in speaking of mutual obedience (RB 71, 1). Therefore, this plan of God, this way, is a mystery of communion:

> By her relationship with Christ, the Church is a kind of sacrament or sign of intimate union with God, and of the unity of all mankind. She is also an instrument for the achievement of such union and unity.... Established by Christ as a fellowship of life, charity, and truth, it is also used by Him as an instrument for the redemption of all (LG 1 and 9).

Fellowship in this ecclesial communion is common to all—we are coresponsible—but we are also all partially blind in respect to God's existential unfolding of His plan for the world's redemption. Besides, God prefers to make use of the natural order of things for the habitual government of this plan. From this flows the need of common information, reflection, prayer, and dialogue, above all when a point of much importance and grave consequences is treated. It is the situation foreseen in RB 3 and 68:

> Let the brothers, then, give their opinions with all submission and humility... If the brother sees that the weight of the command far exceeds his strength, he should suggest to the superior the causes of this impossibility with patience and respect, not with arrogance, resistence, or contradiction. But if after this suggestion, the superior persists in his opinion and command, let

the brother hold for certain that this is to his advantage, and trusting in the help of God, let him obey for the sake of charity.

Its Nature

Dialogued obedience is a way to obey better. The purpose of the exchange of opinions is not to create a democracy, but simply to discover God's will and to relate the common good of the community and the Church to the spiritual good of the individual. *Dialogue presupposes the spirit of obedience*, otherwise it will not be dialogue but escapism and an expression of pride.

The true meaning of the interchange of points of view between a superior and a subject has to be seen under the light of faith. The Church of Christ is not so much an army as a family. The authority is full of love. Respect of persons always takes first place over a plan of action. The hierarchic communion, to which we bind ourselves in a special way by the vow of obedience, has for its model "the unity of the Father, the Son, and the Holy Spirit" (LG 4).

> Let the superior use his authority in a spirit of service for the brothers, and manifest thereby the charity with which God loves them. Governing his subjects as God's own sons, and with regard to their human personality, a superior will make it easier for them to obey gladly.... Let him give the kind of leadership which will encourage religious to bring an active and responsible obedience to the offices they shoulder and the activities they undertake. Therefore, a superior should listen willingly to his subjects and encourage them to make a personal contribution to the welfare of the community and of the Church. Not to be weakened, however, is the superior's authority to decide what be done and to require the doing of it (PC 14).

Although these words are directed principally to superiors, nonetheless they describe the atmosphere and the spirit in which obedience ought to be exercised. The responsibility of creating such an atmosphere falls, above all, on the superiors.

Paul VI expressed the nature of dialogued obedience with even more clarity in his encyclical, *Ecclesiam Suam*:

> We desire to give to the interior relations of the Church the character of a dialogue among members of a body whose constitutive principle is charity. This does not do away with the exercise of the virtue of obedience, since the right order necessary in any well-constructed society, and above all, the hierarchic constitution of the Church require that, on the one hand, authority should be exercised according to its proper function and, on the other hand, there should be submission.... By obedience, therefore, in the context of dialogue, we mean the exercise of authority in the full awareness

of its being a service and ministry of truth and charity, and we mean the observance of Church regulations and respect for the government of legitimate superiors in a spirit of serene availability as becomes free and loving children (118-119).

This is dialogued obedience! Authority's command and human dignity are united in the dynamism of the total gift of self to the love of Christ. Compare these words of Paul VI with the citation from RB 3 and 68 on the preceding page. Note the many common elements: authority, submission, reverence, and serenity, ending in free and loving obedience.

Qualities of Dialogue

In the exercise of obedience and authority, the central point of convergence is a *common search for the will of God*. The plan of the Heavenly Father and the holiness of *all* consist in this. A very positive result of the state of vowed obedience is the effort it demands to enter into the common and total good of the plan of redemption. The quality of our obedience is proportional to the quality of our discernment of God's will. Thus obedience is very far from being a passive attitude, a kind of mutilation of personality. On the contrary, it presupposes an act of the intelligence and a serious interior effort to cooperate with the plan of action approved by the superior or the community. As we have just seen, obedience itself not only permits us to present respectful suggestions to the superior or to the community as a whole, but imposes on us the duty to do so.

On a deeper level, the *interior effort* necessary to obey and cooperate with authority presupposes an interior life of union with God in prayer. *A man of prayer is the only person who can truly practice dialogued obedience*. Really, how can we speak about God's saving plan if we have not meditated on it and made it alive in our own soul? Without this quality of personal intimacy with Christ, dialogue will end up in a spirit of contradiction, escapism, and open disobedience.

In practice, how should it be carried out?

-Be faithful to the *life of prayer*, thus you will cultivate a living faith which will indicate to you when to be silent and when to dialogue.

-When any brother asks something of you, *listen*, try to understand what he wants and grasp his point of view. The life of obedience requires much more intelligence than is generally supposed.

-*Do* what the brother, the superior, or the community has requested, provided there is nothing that appears illogical in it or manifestly contradictory to other expressions of God's will. Do not accustom yourself *always* to suggest what seems better to you. This would betray a certain lack of interior freedom.

-If there is something illogical in what has been asked of you, or something that very probably the superior has not taken into account, *tell it to him*, especially if it is something important, for example, sufficient to prejudice the whole project. You can be certain that this interchange of points of view takes nothing from the value of your obedience. The important thing is to speak briefly and to *speak well*, that is to say, with serenity, humility, clarity, and charity. In a dialogue, our manner of speaking, our attitude, and spirit of cooperation frequently carry more weight than the ideas we try to express.

-If the superior maintains his original request after some minutes of dialogue, try to make that *act of faith and confidence* to which Saint Benedict exhorts us in RB 68: "Let the brother hold for certain that this is for his welfare, and trusting in the help of God, let him obey for the sake of charity."

-We have every right and at times the duty to return at another time to the superior or to the community and to *explain more fully the different points of view*, but always with the qualities of a dialogue between friends: affability, adaptation to the other, tranquillity, and respect. Always be ready to change your opinion.

For the sincere monk, it is inevitable that there be a certain tension between dialogued obedience and humility. But let us remember that the dialogue between the superior and the brother can very easily come to be a form of spiritual direction, that is to say, an expression of humility. Besides, the whole message of RB 68 is that you can exercise humility *within* dialogue, and that dialogue ends with the triumph of obedience. Let us ask the advice of our superiors concerning the type of dialogue they want. Much depends on the desires of each particular superior and the mentality of the community as a whole.

For Further Reflection

1. Can I in conscience follow a command which I consider to be imprudent? What should I do?

2. Does the vow of obedience find any application in the daily tasks of monastic or religious life? Or does it come into play only with explicit commands?

3. What is the relation, in theory and in practice, between Superior and Community? Is it true to say that we obey the community?

Bibliography

Braso, G. *Sentier de Vie*. Begrolles: Abbaye de Bellefontaine, 1974, pp. 153-196.

de Vogue, A. *La Communaute et L'Abbe dans la Regle de Saint Benoit*. Paris: Desclee de Brouwer, 1961, esp. pp. 266-288 and 528-538.

Hausherr, I., et al. *The Theology of Obedience*. London: Supplement to *The Way*, 1968.

Heijke, J. *An Ecumenical Light on Renewal of Religious Community Life: Taize*. Pittsburgh: Duquesne Univ. Press, 1967, pp. 84-112.

Howe, R. L. *The Miracle of Dialogue*. New York: Seabury, 1963.

Louf, A. *Teach us to Pray*, pp. 23-32.

McKenzie, J. *Authority in the Church*. New York: Sheed and Ward, 1965.

Merton, T. *Contemplation in a World of Action*, pp. 117-128 and 269-293.

Orsy, L. *Probing the Spirit: A Theological Evaluation of Communal Discernment*. Denville, New Jersey: Dimension Books, 1976.

Peifer, C. *Monastic Spirituality*, pp. 272-292.

Rahner, K., et al. *Obedience and the Church*. Cleveland: Corpus Books, 1968.

Rees, D., et al. *Consider Your Call*, pp. 84-93 and 189-204.

Suenens, L. J. (Cardinal) *A New Pentecost?* New York: Seabury, 1975, esp. pp. 1-32.

CHAPTER SIX

STABILITY

Stability is the first element named by Saint Benedict in his treatment of monastic profession. The reason for this is that the asceticism of the monastic life, expressed in the vow of conversion of life and stimulated by obedience, would lose much of its purifying efficacy if the monk were constantly wandering from one monastery to another.

It has been said that this vow is one of Benedict's most original additions to the traditional concept of the monastic life. Yet stability was always a key virtue for the monk. If the brother embraces a life of conversion and obedience in imitation of Christ, he ought to carry it through "unto death." Stability is nothing else than perseverance in obedience. The merit of Saint Benedict consists in underlining the importance of stability in the very ceremony of profession and relating it with the community life of the brothers. In the following pages we shall first look at the minimal and rather juridical obligations of the vow, as we have done in previous chapters. Then we can go on to penetrate its full meaning.

The basic obligation of our promise of stability is simple: *By the vow of stability the monk commits himself to live in the community of his profession all his life, unto death.* This is the foundation of what follows.

1. THE COMMITMENT

This promise of stability is specifically monastic. It is not a question of stability in the religious *state*, or in our own *Order*, nor of perseverance in the practice of the *monastic observances* in a general way, but of *local stability* in the community of profession. Even more precisely it means perseverance in the *monastic life of this community*, that is to say, in the dynamism of renunciation and conversion which is the reason for its existence.

Different Interpretations

In the history of monasticism stability has been lived in various ways:

-Stability in the cell. This is the primitive sense of monastic stability, a remedy and a weapon against the temptation to roam or to visit the cell of another brother. It is an ascetic practice which forms part of monastic discipline but without being the object of an explicit promise, much less of a vow with a juridic obligation. It is the point of view of the Desert Fathers and Cassian.

-Stability under an abbot who could have several houses under his jurisdiction. This was the practice at Cluny in the eleventh and twelfth centuries as well as in the Benedictine and Cistercian Congregations which maintained stability to the Congregation or Province. A monk could observe his vow of stability in any house of the Congregation. This is a broad interpretation.

-Stability "on the pillar." To remain always in one and the same monastery without going to another house under any pretext. This interpretation was carried to its limit by some hermits who chained themselves to the walls of their caves or were enclosed in one room until death; or by some monks of Syria who passed their entire lives on the top of a pillar. A very exceptional vocation!

-Stability of a traveler. In some monastic Congregations one is a member of a determined community for life, but in practice travels to other places and lives temporarily in other monasteries.

-Stability in the community. This is the interpretation of Saint Benedict: to live in the community of profession for all one's life, until death, only traveling outside the monastery as an exception. It implies not changing to another community without a special reason, e.g., a foundation, the command of the superior, physical or spiritual health. This seems to have been the mind of Saint Pachomius in the fourth century. It is the traditional interpretation of the Cistercians and of many Benedictine Congregations. This is the stability which we are treating here.

Benedictine Stability

The central promise of Benedictine stability is to live with the community until death. The vow binds us to the *community*, not necessarily to the place and much less to the person of the abbot.

According to RB 58, the principal result of profession is that the novice is "admitted into the community" (*suscipiatur in congregatione...in congregatione reputetur* — RB 58, 14 and 23). This is the significance of the kiss of peace which takes place immediately after having made profession: "Then let the novice prostrate himself before the feet of each monk, asking him to pray for him; and from that day let him be counted as one of the community" (RB 58, 23).

It is clear from the last verse of the Rule's Prologue that this belonging to the community has implications which are both ascetic and mystical: "Thus, never abandoning our Master but persevering in his teaching in the monastery unto death, we shall share by patience in the sufferings of Christ, that we may deserve to be partakers also of his kingdom" (Prol., 50).

Chapters 4 to 7 of the Rule propose the principal elements of this divine teaching in which the monk must persevere. At the end of Chapter 4, on the tools of good works, Saint Benedict again indicates the ultimate end of stability: "What God has prepared for those who love Him" (RB 4, 76-77). He then clearly distinguishes stability from enclosure: "Now the workshop where he shall diligently execute all these tasks, is the enclosure of the monastery and stability in the community" (RB 4, 78).

This last quotation is important. According to Saint Benedict, remaining in the enclosure of the monastery is something different from stability. The former looks to physical withdrawal from society and pertains rather to conversion of life, whereas Benedictine stability refers to being a permanent member of the group of persons who live within that enclosure. Stability is something personal. It is interpersonal communion or, to put it better, it is perseverance in this communion, that is to say, in the dynamism of renunciation and conversion to the love of Christ that constitutes the heart of the monastic community.

For example, the brother who leaves the enclosure in order to enjoy himself at the house of a neighbor without any permission would offend against the vow of conversion of life, but would not directly break his promise of stability since he remains a member of the community.

Nevertheless, on the positive side, it would be difficult to fulfill the profound spiritual exigencies of conversion of life without putting into practice the letter and spirit of stability. This is an example of how the different vows mutually compenetrate each other, as we have already seen in the relation between obedience and conversion of life (see Chapter Five). Likewise, stability is an expression of the spirit of consecrated virginity, poverty, and obedience.

Infidelities to the Promise

When, then, is there a direct offense against stability?

-*Exteriorly*, by desertion or apostasy, that is to say, the illegitimate departure from the monastery with the intention of not returning; or, having left with permission, remaining outside of the monastery with the intention of removing oneself from religious obedience. The deserter thus sins against three vows at once: conversion of life, obedience, and stability.

One can be unfaithful, also in a serious manner, by fleeing without permission to another monastery with the intention of not returning to one's own community. If the intention is to return later, the infidelity would be against the norms of enclosure and the promise of obedience. Of course it would be against the *spirit* of stability.

-*Interiorly*, one can offend against stability by the determination to obtain an indult of exclaustration or of change of stability to another monastery without sufficient reason. Care should be taken to avoid romantic thoughts about a "better place." Such vague daydreaming is an imperfection and constitutes an obstacle against entrance into the spirit of the vow. We shall return to this point later.

-*Indirectly*, one can go against the vow by threatening desertion in order to gain a special permission from the superiors. If made with full deliberation to fulfill the threat, this would be a grave offense against the vow. But not if the threat were made in a moment of nervous excitement.

2. SPECIAL CASES WHEN ONE CAN LEAVE ONE COMMUNITY AND ENTER ANOTHER

A Foundation

By making his promise of stability, the monk is united to a community and gives himself to it to serve it in whatever capacity the superiors might desire. Stability implies not merely remaining in one place, but also identifying oneself with the community for life, in all its works, its ups and downs, its tensions, its joys, and its sorrows. Establishing a daughter house is one of the most important and significant works in the life of a community. All cooperate to prepare a foundation by the fervor of their monastic life, and likewise all can be in part responsible for the failure of the most beautiful projects by their repeated irregularities. If one day the foundation is approved, only certain of the brothers will go to it, but the whole community, with its prayers and sacrifices, will contribute to the new implantation of monastic life, undertaken by the chosen group in the name of the whole community.

Being a member of the group that goes on the foundation, far from going contrary to the vow of stability, fulfills it and transcends it. Some advantages of the established life, such as complete regularity and greater structural security, are sacrificed in order to bring to fulfillment a work desired by the community.

In practice, however, it is possible that the occasion of a foundation—or any other need in the Order—be used to "escape" from a difficult or burdensome situation in one's own community. We can try to resolve a problem of obedience by means of a change of environment and of superiors, when in reality the cause of the problem is in ourselves. We carry our problems with us. So we should proceed with caution in offering ourselves for a foundation, and superiors should resist the temptation to rid themselves of such and such a brother or sister by sending them to a foundation. Some suggestions:

-If we want to go to a daughter house or help in regard to other needs of the Order, we must be sure that we are not dealing with an escape or flight on our part, covering under the mantle of sacrifice what in reality is a surrender to temptation.

-The positive and spontaneous approbation of someone with spiritual authority should precede the official request to go.

-The decision remains in the hands of the superior, and our manner of procedure ought to be humble and full of abandonment. If he says no, or places reasons against it, we should accept them tranquilly and cheerfully as the will of God, and forget the matter.

-In general, it is better not to offer our services until they are clearly asked for. Nonetheless, at times one can take the initiative, but the reasons ought to be so much the stronger and our attitude so much the more detached.

Obedience

The monk can be sent to another monastery for some years, for example, as a worker, as chaplain to nuns, as superior, or as a student. When the initiative comes from the superiors, there is no problem. Neither the letter nor the spirit of the vow of stability is violated. Everything is directed by obedience. However, if the monk actively seeks one of these positions in another house, especially as an escape from frustrations at home, he probably fails in the spirit of stability.

Health

A stay of some weeks or months in a hospital does not affect the promise of stability, but is health a sufficient reason for moving permanently from one community to another?

If it is clearly seen that a permanent change to another monastery, with a different climate, *will notably better and even cure* completely the health problems of a monk who is unwell in his own community, then a change of stability would be not only legitimate, but also highly recommended—under the condition that other factors, especially spiritual ones, do not enter into play.

Nonetheless, it is only in really special cases, when the doctor has recommended the move for objectively founded reasons, that we should think of a change of stability. There is much room for illusion in this matter. Our instinct should be to reject as temptations such thoughts of a "better place," believing firmly that God sanctifies us in the midst of tribulations. The Council itself has said: "Communities of contemplative life have a very great importance in the conversion of souls by their prayers, works of penance, and tribulations" (AG 40).

Let us be careful, then, not to try to escape when tribulations present themselves, but ask for the faith to embrace Jesus who calls us many times by means of tribulations and in the midst of them.

A Greater Spiritual Good

If stability can be changed for reasons of physical health, one can also, in theory, change it for reasons of spiritual health: going to another house or another Order where one would be able to open himself up more fully to God and attain a deeper union with Him.

Nevertheless, it must be recognized that one of the principal reasons of the vow of stability is to guard against the temptation to seek a greater good in another place or community. The promise of stability is based on the fact that the monk, under the appearance of a greater good, can follow a path which would make him lose the positive good which he already has and, in the end, completely lose his religious vocation.

The other vows foster resistance to more or less evident evils: sinful pleasure, self-will, an easy, worldly life, the amassing of possessions. Stability is directed against the possibility of an evil disguised as a spiritual good.

In itself, the vow makes it impossible for a monk to change his community; but the purpose of the vow is to make him realize that *stability itself is an immense good,* and that in the vast majority of cases it constitutes a much greater good than that which might be attained by a change to another community or Order. If a monk maintains stability, he will be able to effect the great change which alone is important: change within himself, transformation into Christ, full openness to the Holy Spirit. If we seek satisfaction somewhere else, we are not going to work to attain the good which can be ours here and now.

Therefore, the vow of stability implies, of itself, renouncing the thought of seeking a greater good, even a greater spiritual good, in another community.

Thus, it is necessary to deal carefully with all thoughts concerning a change of community. We can fail against the vow of stability by deliberately thinking about a change to another house when we believe that such a thought is a temptation. But with openness and docility to a spiritual father there is probably no infidelity.

When is it advisable to change stability for a greater spiritual good?

Transfer to Another House

In spite of what we have said, it can happen that another monastery might really be better for the spiritual development of an individual. In general, this problem ought to be seriously studied *before* solemn profession, but if a spiritual father and the superior agree that it might be best, then it is certainly licit, and probably advisable, to ask for a change of stability, even after profession. However, the conditions which follow are important:

The desire to change stability ought not to be a sudden whim. It ought to be tested, especially over the course of time.

-He who desires to change should be a mature man of firm character.

-It should not be a question of self-will, but of submission to obedience. The brother should show by a humble reception of the decisions of others that his motives are supernatural.

-It should not be an escape. The normal problems of community life must be confronted, not avoided. One who questions his monastic vocation seldom saves it by changing to another community.

Nonetheless, it can happen that some personalities adapt to the environment of one monastery better than to that of another. You can have a vocation to a small community, and not to a very large one; to a house in your own country, and not in a mission country. But in practice, these problems ought to be resolved before monastic profession. After profession, everything favors keeping stability.

Transfer to Another Contemplative Order

In theory, we ought not to seek to change to another Order unless it is to a more perfect and strict life. In practice, even this change has many inconveniences. It is one thing to transfer from an active Order, for example, the Salesians or Redemptorists, to a contemplative one. But it is another thing to pass from one contemplative Order to another which is also contemplative, such as the Carthusians or the Camaldolese. The Church does not easily grant this change, nor do the superiors of the Orders involved look on it very favorably.

Even in the cases when monks have tried to enter into other Orders, for example, on termination of simple vows, it has often happened that they have failed in the other Order and thus have lost what they had without gaining anything. At times they lost everything. It is certainly dangerous.

The Eremitical Life Within a Cenobitic Order

It is common that a local superior can give permission to a monk, whom he judges to have the necessary qualities, to live a more solitary life *within* the property of the monastery. This possibility, which reflects the situation described in RB 1, 3-5, makes a change to another contemplative Order much less necessary.

In itself, the life of a hermit who lives apart from the community, but under the control of the abbot, is not opposed to the promise of stability. The hermit continues to belong to the community. He can even be a symbol and witness to the brethren of the values that are at the center of every monastic vocation: the exclusive search for God, continual prayer, separation from men in order to be present to them all in the Heart of Christ.

But a vocation to the eremitical life, even within our Order, is very exceptional. The candidate for such a life not only must combine qualities of maturity, obedience, balance, spirit of prayer, application to manual labor, and fraternal charity, but also must feel that he lacks some *important element* in his life of prayer which he cannot obtain within the horarium and environment of the monastery. *Positive* signs are necessary for this special vocation.

Transfer to the Active Apostolate or to the Lay State

Can this be for the greater spiritual good of a monk or nun? According to Saint Thomas Aquinas, the mixed life, where you give to others the fruits of your own contemplation, is higher than the purely "contemplative" life (ST II-II, 188, 6). In practice, however, a religious passes from Orders of the "mixed" life, such as the Dominicans or Jesuits, to the monastic state as to a somehow "higher" life. It would be rare that a monk who has adapted well to his vocation, encounter his "greater spiritual good" in the apostolic ministry. A truly extraordinary sign, for example, from the Holy See, or in some way from God Himself, would be necessary in order to try such a change, since the latter would be not only contrary to stability, but also against conversion of life.

In a particular case, a person who has not adapted well to the monastic life might change—and at times he ought to change—to the active life. The difficulty in such cases is probably rooted in the lack of a true monastic vocation, the absence of which was not recognized until it was too late.

3. SPIRIT OF STABILITY

Why do we make the promise of stability? Does it not seem to be against the spirit of detachment and favor a life of comfort? And how is such a static concept compatible with the need for constant psychological growth and human development? Is it really healthy and sufficient to remain in the monastery unto death?

These questions are especially important for us when we ask ourselves, whether as an individual or as a group, "What am I? What must I do? What is my function in the world and in the people of God?" Now, stability is one of the most typical elements of the monastic life as conceived by Saint Benedict, although it is not the most important. Charity, obedience, and conversion of life, are certainly more important and unite us more directly to God. But in order to understand the proper identity of the monastic vocation, the mission which the monk fulfills in the world, and what distinguishes the monastic calling from all other forms of life in the Church, it is necessary to deepen our appreciation of the spirit of stability. A brief look at monastic tradition will help us to grasp this spirit and to see the vow's deep Christian meaning.

Monastic Stability According to the Desert Fathers

Among the Desert Fathers there were pilgrim monks such as Abba Bessarion who went about from place to place, imitating literally those heroes of the Old Testament whose description we find in Heb. 11:37-38: "They went about in sheepskins and goatskins, destitute, distressed, afflicted—of whom the world was not worthy—wandering in deserts, mountains, caves, and holes in the earth."

But many other Fathers put great importance on remaining in the cell:

Remain in your cell and your cell will teach you everything.

Just as a tree cannot bear fruit when it is transplanted frequently, likewise a monk cannot bear fruit if he often changes his dwelling.

When a man dwells in a place and produces no fruit in it, the place itself casts him out as one who has not borne fruit.

It is worth the effort to meditate on these sayings. We find a similar teaching in the emphasis placed by Zen Buddhist monks on remaining seated during meditation. The restless monk believes that he must change his place in order to be more perfect, but really he does nothing more than justify his sterility in the community of which he is a member. He has borne no fruit and thinks he should go elsewhere, but it is the monastery itself that acts on him to "cast him out." The situation is dangerous. He could lose his vocation and even all religious meaning to his life. The remedy is not in going to another place, but in opening himself to truth, love, and self-sacrifice in the place where he is. The basic fact is that there is a close bond between fruitfulness and stability.

Once someone asked Abba Anthony: "What must I do in order to please God?" The old man answered: "Remember my teaching and these words. Wherever you go, preserve the remembrance of God. Whatever you do, do it according to the norm of Holy Scripture. And wherever you live, do not be hasty to change your place of residence. If you keep these rules, you will be saved."

In this "word of salvation" Saint Anthony does not categorically forbid a change of place, but says that it should not be done lightly, without serious motivation. This is the spirit of our vow.

Monastic stability, of itself, means renouncing the thought of seeking a greater good, even a greater spiritual good, in another community. For this reason, at times of trial when the temptation comes to go to another place, or when those nostalgic and romantic thoughts about an "ideal setup" appear, it is necessary to reject such ideas. The trial must be faced here. Benedictine stability places us in a situation where sooner or later we arrive at the heart of every human situation—the choice between despair and the total gift of self to God. It is an identity crisis at the deepest level of our being. Human nature tries by every means possible to escape this fundamental choice. A change of place will not help much.

The Fathers used to say: If a temptation arises where you are living in the desert, don't leave your dwelling in the hour of temptation. For if you go at that moment, you will encounter the same temptation awaiting you wherever you go. Be patient until the temptation goes away, so that your departure may not scandalize the brothers who live in the same place nor cause them anguish.

In this text, we find another important aspect of stability. It is not only a question of the good of the monk himself, but also something which affects others. Scandal and bad example must be avoided. When a monk embraces the monastic state, he engages himself in the presence of the entire community (the local church) and of all men (the universal Church) to persevere in the practice of asceticism in a given place and with a specific community. Such a promise cannot be broken without truly serious reasons.

One more reference to the Fathers of the Desert: Abba Anthony used to say, "Humility is the country to which the Lord wants us to go and offer our sacrifice."

Perhaps this metaphor was Anthony's answer to the question of a monk who wished to change his dwelling in order to be more pleasing to the Lord. The wise man prefers humility and conversion to pilgrimage. It is precisely this point of view that Saint Benedict follows in his Rule (RB 71, 1). The same detachment from created things which was symbolized and brought about by moving from one place to another in the desert is achieved better, with more security and efficacy, by persevering in one place and accepting the monastic way of life, especially obedience. For the monk of Saint Benedict, obedience is the best way to make a pilgrimage, i.e., to go to God. Stability and pilgrimage thus have the same ascetic purpose.

Monastic Stability According to the First Cistercians

The nature of monastic stability is greatly clarified by the writings of the early Cistercians. They applied the traditional doctrine to the case of monks of the twelfth century who wished to change their monastery and embrace the new reform of the white monks.

Saint Bernard prefers Benedictine monks to reform their own monasteries rather than abandon them to enter a Cistercian house (cf. *De Praecepto et Dispensatione*, Ch. 16-18, nn. 44-56). For him, the fundamental principle is that "one is never justified in defaulting when he has promised by vow to do a good act" (n. 44). From this, three consequences follow:

-A change of stability is *illicit* when it flows from a natural restlessness, or when it is a question of entering a house of slack observance (n. 44).

-A change is *licit but rarely to be counseled* when it is a question of changing from one monastery to another, even when the latter may be more austere or observant. And the consent of one's abbot is necessary, as the Rule of Saint Benedict requires. "It is hardly safe to leave a certain good for an uncertain hope...for that which one lightly desires when he does not have it may well become insupportable once experienced. This sort of foolish levity is only too common" (n. 46).

-A change is *advisable and advised* when it is a question of passing from a truly relaxed and corrupt house where bad example is given, to a really good and observant community: "I would counsel him to move to some other place under the guidance of the Spirit of liberty, where he may be more free to live as he has engaged himself by vow to do" (n. 44).

William of St. Thierry, in Chapter 3 of the first part of the *Golden Epistle*, gives the ascetic principles of stability. No one can live a life of prayer and recollection while changing monasteries frequently. Man cannot concentrate the powers of the mind if he does not root his body in a fixed place. The remedy for infirmities of the soul is not a change of place but a change of heart.

William underlines a new and important aspect of monastic stability: *docility in spiritual direction.* It is not sufficient to remain in the same place; it is also necessary to be under the direction of a spiritual teacher. Personal knowledge and spiritual guidance require time. The prescription consists in stability, tranquillity, solitude, and obedience.

Blessed Guerric of Igny develops the same themes, applying to stability the parable of the sower (Lk. 8:13). The Word of God falls on rocky ground: at the beginning it is accepted with joy, but it does not grow for *lack of roots.* Stability is necessary to permit the divine vocation to take root in the heart. This is especially so for the contemplative vocation to experimental knowledge of God built upon charity:

Happy the man who lives with Wisdom (Ecclus. 14:22). The proud of heart reject wisdom when they meet her. Others, like Solomon, let themselves be drawn by the delights of the flesh. Still others, losing themselves in trifles or inconstancy of mind, abandon her, being put out by the slightest difficulty. They believe for a time but when temptation comes they turn to other things. But why do they abandon her? Because they have not sunk roots to stabilize themselves. And how can they sink roots if they do not remain in the same place? Truly, the just man planted in the House of the Lord can become rooted and built upon charity only by permanence and stability in the same place (*First Sermon for the Feast of Saint Benedict*).

We can see here how *concrete and objective* the monastic spirit is. For a monk it does not suffice to have good intentions and to be disposed to live with the brethren until death. Let reality prove the sincerity of his dispositions and intentions! Let him remain stabilized in his own community. Then we shall see if he really is willing to live with them or if, on the contrary, he is simply waxing romantic with beautiful words about brotherly love.

A genuine monastic vocation is not necessarily connected with great initial fervor. To begin well is a grace from God, but how many begin well and are very promising, but do not persevere! Perseverance is the proof of an authentic generosity which does not wither under the difficulties, routine, and monotony of community life. An apparently ordinary spirituality which follows its course to the end is much better than one which begins brilliantly, perhaps with applause from the grandstand, but which stops half way.

Blessed Guerric finishes by saying that very rarely would he counsel a change of monastery, even though this could help some people. In general, he thinks that the desire for a change comes from impatience, restlessness, and illusions of the imagination.

Doctrinal Reflections

We have seen that monastic literature, from the Sayings of the Desert Fathers up to Blessed Guerric, uses the image of a fruitful tree to show the need for stability. Just as a tree or a grain of wheat does not produce fruit unless it first puts its roots down into the earth, likewise the monk will not grow in love if he does not sink roots in his cell (eremitical life) or in his community (cenobitic life). The image comes directly from the Bible:

-The people of Israel are the vineyard of the Lord which has not brought forth fruit (Is. 5:1-7; Ps. 79:9-20; Mt. 21:33-43).

-The just man is like a tree with his roots in the Law of the Lord (Ps. 1:3; Jer. 17:7-8).

-It is not advisable to change dwellings (Prov. 27:8; Ecclus. 29:22-27).

-Jesus applies this teaching to his disciples: "The seed is the Word of God.... The seed on good ground are those who hear the Word in a spirit of openness, retain it, and bear fruit through perseverance" (Lk. 8:11-15).

-"I am the true vine and my Father is the Vinegrower.... Abide in me as I abide in you. As the branch cannot bear fruit of itself unless it remain on the vine, so neither can you unless you abide in me. I am the vine, you are the branches. He who abides in me and I in him will produce abundantly" (Jn. 15:1-17).

This entire passage from the discourse of the Last Supper represents the peak of the spirit of monastic stability. *The whole purpose of the vow of stability is to attain this stability in love*, that is to say, stability in living the Word of God. This is the kingdom of Christ, the meaning of a monastic community.

Certainly there are many roads which lead to the abiding love of Christ, according to the variety of vocations in the Church. But to bind oneself permanently to a community of brothers and to a particular material place, corresponds to that connaturality between the material and the spiritual which is at the heart of monasticism and of each particular monastic vocation. Monastic asceticism follows an overall principle according to which *the spiritual life should find its expression and its support in the external order*. Interior humility, which in other persons may be compatible with external honors, must be concretized for the monk in a humble state of life. Similarly, night vigils express the spiritual vigilance to which every Christian is called. Fasting and abstinence should both reveal and foster purity of heart.

This ascetic principle also applies to stability. All men are called to abide in the love of Christ. Christian life consists precisely in this. But the dynamism at the heart of the monastic way of life calls for an expression, a means, and an embodiment of this spiritual abiding. The soul of monasticism is to anticipate here and now, insofar as possible, the eternal life of heaven, and to establish the kingdom of God in the whole man—body and soul. This brings with it the intrinsic need of bodily stability which corresponds to fidelity in love.

Thus, like the other vows, the promise of stability does nothing more than make clear and explicit what is already within the basic thrust of the monastic vocation—to establish the kingdom of God and bring to completion the history of salvation. By means of bodily stability, not only does the monk himself have a greater guarantee of arriving at an abiding love of Christ, but the whole Church also receives a tangible witness of her own essential vocation—to be the faithful bride of Christ.

Fidelity! The whole drama of Salvation History is summed up in the theme of fidelity to the Covenant. God, Yahweh, is always faithful— "His mercy endures forever"—but his people do not remain faithful to their God. All through the Old Testament, Yahweh seeks this fidelity and finds it only in a small group of His people. They are the remnant of Israel, the Poor of Yahweh, led and personified by the mysterious Servant of the Lord:

> I have not rebelled, have not turned back. I gave my back to those who beat me, my cheeks to those who plucked my beard; my face I did not shield from buffets and spitting. The Lord God is my help, therefore I am not disgraced. I have set my face like flint, knowing that I shall not be put to shame (Is. 50:5-7).

By means of the work of Christ and the humble faithfulness of Mary, humanity is established once and for all in fidelity to its spouse, the Son of God. This is the mission of the Holy Spirit:

> I will pray to the Father and He will give you another Paraclete who will remain with you always.... You will see me because I live and you will live. That day you will understand that I am in my Father and that you are in me and I in you (Jn. 14:16-20).

Heaven will be the consummation of this reciprocal fidelity between God and man. In the Book of Revelation 21:1-7, we see not only the reward for monastic stability, but also its meaning, its spirit, and its exemplar: the holy and eternal city, the faithful bride, the dwelling place of God, the eternal Covenant, new heavens and a new earth, Christ the beginning and the end.

The Second Vatican Council sketches the traits of the Church's pilgrimage toward this eternal stability. The description can well be applied to the life of monastic stability:

> Moving forward through trial and tribulation, the Church is strengthened by the power of God's grace promised to her by the Lord, so that in the weakness of the flesh she may not waver from perfect fidelity, but remain a bride worthy of her Lord; and moved by the Holy Spirit, she may never cease to renew herself, until through the cross she arrives at the light which knows no setting (LG 9).

Person and Community

Our promise of stability reflects so faithfully the mystery of the Church, the Spouse of Christ, that it is necessary to clarify the specifically monastic and ascetic meaning of the vow. Moreover, some modern writers have abused the relation between the heavenly Jerusalem and the religious community by finding almost all the meaning of the religious vows in their communal aspect. The vows would be in the first place means to establish the *perfect Christian community*; and only secondarily, means to sanctify the person involved.

Such a viewpoint seems to put the plow before the horse, since the whole purpose of a religious community is the transformation in Christ of each of its members. This *is* the common good. Community is for the persons who make it up. Thus, stability in the community is not primarily for the perfecting of the community in the sense of making it more orderly and stable, but rather in order to *root the monk in the search for God and in the fulfillment of the plan of the Father*. Fraternal love and Christian community spring from this personal search and achievement.

This personal orientation is far from being the product of egotistic individualism. It is simply the consequence of the inner nature of a vocation to the service of God. The monastic vocation, as described in the Prologue of the RB, is a *very personal dialogue between Christ and the monk*. The present development of the theology of vocation supports this viewpoint. Following the call of the Lord, the monk joins a group of men, receives spiritual direction, good example, a life of prayer, and, above all, the love needed to deepen his dialogue with Christ and to enter fully into the kingdom of God. The community is at the service of its members, not as though they were simply members of a club, but because they are *persons loved by God*.

The teaching of the Church concerning society in general ought also to be applied to the monastic community:

> The social order and its progressive development must at every moment be subordinate to the good of the human person if the disposition of affairs is to be subjected to the personal realm and not contrariwise, as the Lord indicated when He said that the Sabbath was made for man, and not man for the Sabbath.... The ferment of the Gospel, too, has aroused and continues to arouse in man's heart the irresistible requirements of his dignity (GS 26).

Having said this, it is certain, nevertheless, that the vows taken as a whole, and stability in a very special way, have a close relation to the community of brothers. We saw this at the beginning of the present chapter in reference to Saint Benedict's approach to stability. Vatican II uncovers the doctrinal roots of this approach, teaching that:

> God did not create man to live in isolation, but for the formation of social unity. Likewise, God has willed to sanctify and save men not separately, with the exclusion of all mutual relationship, but constituted them a people that might recognize Him in truth and serve Him holily. From the beginning of the history of salvation, God has chosen men not only as individuals, but also as members of a determined community.... This communitarian character is developed and consummated in the work of Jesus Christ (GS 32).

How can we find the proper balance between personal dignity and the more or less structured society in which we live? Between our deepest vocation to an intimate relation with Christ and the social duties of common life?

There is no other way than the gift of self—*love*—a generous, humble, and respectful love. This is why the Council, after having spoken about the dignity of the human person, says:

> Coming down to practical and particularly urgent consequences, this Council lays stress on reverence for man; everyone must consider his every neighbor without exception as another self, taking into account first of all his life and the means to living it with dignity (GS 27).

How can we love God if we do not love our brothers? The community from which each one has a right to receive direction, example, help, and love is not an abstraction. By becoming a member of the community and above all by making a promise of stability, we take upon ourselves the responsibility of offering our brothers every possible help, both material and spiritual. In doing this it is, in the first place, we ourselves who grow in perfection as persons and as sons of God: "Give and it will be given to you" (Lk. 6:38).

We may call the vow of stability the *commitment to fraternal love*—to the *philia* which we saw as a dimension of Christian chastity—since to abide and to bear fruit in the love of Christ (*agape*) means to love one's brothers. For the monk, the local community is like a sacrament of the people of God on pilgrimage toward heaven, a charismatic and hierarchical communion of faith, hope, and love. While the life of obedience focuses especially on the hierarchical and charismatic aspects of community, the life of stability unites us directly with the communion, that is, the *koinonia*—the sharing of spiritual and material goods which occurs in the society of the baptized, the Body of Christ (LG 13). It is the life of the primitive Church, described in the first chapters of Acts. This material and spiritual fellowship is not an end in itself, but a dynamism, an attitude, an environment that reflects the generosity of God toward His adopted sons and ultimately expresses the self-giving of the Father to the Son in the Holy Spirit.

Such is the meaning of cenobitic stability. The purpose of this deep communion is the development in the best way possible of the personal vocation of each brother. True fraternal fellowship will spring spontaneously from the fullness of the Spirit's action in the heart of each monk.

For this reason, when Saint Benedict describes the life of the monastic community, he is pointing to the spirit of stability:

> Let the monks, therefore, exercise this zeal with the most fervent love.... Let them bear with the greatest patience one another's infirmities.... Let them

vie in paying obedience one to another. Let none follow what seems good for himself, but rather what is good for another. Let them practice fraternal charity with a pure love. Let them fear God. Let them love their abbot with a sincere and humble affection. Let them prefer nothing whatever to Christ. And may He bring us all alike to life everlasting (RB 72, 3-12).

It is only in the context of abiding in this fraternal love that the monk is going to find his share in the cross of Christ which will purify and sanctify him: "Persevering in the Lord's teaching in the monastery until death, we shall share by patience in the sufferings of Christ, so that we may deserve to be partakers also of his kingdom" (RB Prol., 50).

This text puts the last touch on the monastic doctrine of stability according to Saint Benedict. In the other passages of the Rule, cited at the beginning of this chapter, the object of stability is the incorporation into the *congregatio*, i.e., into the community as Christ's sheepfold under the guidance of the abbot as Christ's vicar. According to this last text, however, the object of the monk's perseverance is "the Lord's teaching." But what is this teaching if not love, the new Commandment, the *agape* which Jesus brought with him to the world from the bosom of the Father in order to communicate it to men, purify by it all human love, and transform man's love into His own?

Thus, the vow of stability is not only a promise to persevere in the monastery but also, and above all, a promise to persevere in love, in the teaching of Christ, It is personal fidelity to the New Covenant sealed in the Blood of Christ and lived out by this community in this place. Thus every act of personal fidelity to the Word of Christ, and of service or patience toward the brothers, having been consecrated by baptism, is emphasized and favored by the vow.

Another aspect of the spirit of stability is that by its *interpersonal* character it implies, besides the love of the brethren, the love of those who do not persevere, of those who leave the monastery. But who knows? Perhaps their leaving, the difficulties that made them leave, are due to our lack of charity or want of understanding, or lack of humility. Perhaps they received bad example from us. Only God can judge, but let us not be Pharisees. We all share in the stability or instability of the brethren. The best way to avoid departures and defections is to create an atmosphere of fraternal understanding and authentic love.

4. LOVE OF THE ORDER

The life of stability also demands a *sincere love of the Order* to which we belong. It is an essential element of the spirit of stability and at the same time a remedy against instability. What use is there in remaining in the Order while hating it interiorly? It would be better to leave. The presence of monks who do not love their own Order, who do not give themselves with genuine enthusiasm to the life protected and favored by the Order, constitutes a great danger for the perseverance of many vocations. Instead of a climate of contemplative love, those who enter can encounter a spirit of opposition and resentment created by those who react against the institution. It is a serious difficulty and can be diffused more easily precisely because of a greater spontaneity in dialogue which, of itself, is healthy. You become critical, and the danger consists in becoming a fault finder.

But he who is thinking of making a vow of stability unto death in a monastic community ought to assure himself that he has a genuine love of the Order. And if he wants to maintain the spirit of the vow, he must continue to cultivate this love during all his life. He who is going to live his vow of stability fully should take the resolution to do all that is possible to live peacefully and fruitfully in the spirit of his vocation. He should try to be a fruitful and productive member through a life which is deeply spiritual, balanced, happy, and of service both to the community and to the Order or Congregation. His vocation is to be a healthy member of the organism, and not an obstacle full of rebellion.

What is Love of the Order?

It is the full acceptance of this human institution and the gift of oneself to it *as it is.* Loving our community, Congregation, or Order does not imply maintaining, cost what it may, the same idealistic enthusiasm that we had as novices, nor much less that which we had as aspirants. Love of the Order changes and is made deeper with experience. It tends to become more realistic and less sentimental.

There are two difficulties in the love of the Order: a false idealism and a lack of vocation.

Lack of Realism

Idealism blinds us at times to the imperfections of our Order and its members, as if our way of life were to be thought of as the best and the most perfect within the Church. It insists on the "superiority" of the contemplative life over those who lead an active life. It cites the texts of the Council and of recent Popes. It is highly pleased when guests or preachers praise our life or our monastery, when they wax eloquent on our utility for the Church, as if the world depended on us, that we are the salt of the earth, or heroes of the Lord.

Consequently, we who should be the most humble in the Church are in fact frequently very occupied and preoccupied with our own importance, our own dignity, our superiority. It is true that we must study the Order, know its history, its structures, and its spirit. Not, however, in order to boast but rather in order to serve the Church and all men from within our own vocation.

Besides, fixing our attention too much on ourselves is not healthy and in reality often produces a reaction *against* the Order, and justifiably so. But such a reaction also is dangerous, inasmuch as it is directed against the Order and not against the immaturity of some of its members. It can even lead to the loss of a vocation.

This *false love*, then, is the fruit of a childish conviction of our superiority in the Church. By a subtle search for security more than for truth, we try to convince ourselves and others of our own excellence. Instead of causing true security, this desire to excel produces insecurity, aggressiveness, and doubt.

True love accepts the Order as it is. It flees from that desire to be ranked higher than others. Since it is based on the reality of things, it feels a repulsion toward a spirit of boasting. We do not love the Order because it might be theoretically "superior" or "privileged" within the Church, but because it is the sacrament of the mercy of God toward us. It is the *concrete sign of the personal love* that God offers us at each moment, and is at the same moment the *instrument* that God has personally chosen for us in order that we may grow in His love. The Order offers us what our heart has sought and desired: a separation from the tumult of the world and from many of its dangers; a penitential life that aids us to make reparation for our sins and to strengthen our love; silence that permits us to be with God in dialogue; the liturgical life which enriches our days with the grace of Christ and with spiritual joy.

In a word, the Order represents for us that interpretation of the Gospel which best responds to our needs and desires. It gives us invaluable aids for seeking God and finding Him, for living the mysteries of Christ, for living in Christ and centering our lives on Him. In this sense, love of the Order is nothing but love of Jesus Christ, because our way of life is our way to God in Christ, who is the Way.

An authentic love of the Order is not a love of the faults and deficiencies of some of its members. It means a love of the authentic spirit of the Order, of a life which is authentically Cistercian or Benedictine. There can be interior conflict and anguish when a genuine love of the true spirit finds itself frustrated by the lack of this spirit within the community. Yet a certain amount of tension is a sign of life and growth.

Without high ideals and personal convictions concerning basic principles of monastic life the monk will never come to be the person that he is destined to be. He will always be passive, somewhat infantile, out of orbit.

Be realistic. This means *love the Order and your monastery as they are, not only as they should be*, remembering always that subtle form of hypocrisy which condemns the faults of others in order to whitewash one's own lack of generosity, one's own impatience and infidelity to grace.

In practice, we should love the genuine Benedictine-Cistercian ideal and at the same time love the Order and the monastery in the concrete form in which they exist, which can be far from the ideal. We must learn to accept an imperfect situation with a sense of responsibility and work with loyalty to attain the ideal proposed by monastic tradition within the situation created by ourselves, by our brethren, and by others. We must overcome evil with the good of a patient love.

"Idealism," says the Prior of Taize, "is not an evangelical virtue." But generosity is. Often discontented monks are irritated because they do not find in the Order or in the community the inspiration, affection, encouragement, and help that they demand of it, as if in order to be a monk it were enough to let oneself be carried passively by the life of the community.

True love of the Order cannot be based on what we can get from the Order. This is not realistic. It may be sufficient for the first years, but sooner or later we have to make ourselves personally responsible for the spirit which reigns around us. If you want love in your monastic life, put love into your monastic life. Thus you will draw love from it. But if you only hope that the life "will do you good" or "will make you happy," you will be deceived.

Love of the monastic life demands generosity toward the monastic life. Love of the monastic community requires that we make ourselves servants of everyone.

LACK OF A GENUINE VOCATION

This is the deepest cause of difficulties in loving the Order or in accepting its concrete manifestation in our local community. A true love presupposes a true vocation to the search for God as a monk or nun. When, during the period of formation, the vocation is not profoundly tested, it is inevitable that there be men and women within the Order who are incapable of loving it, since they have not been truly called to it by Christ.

Is our own vocation genuine? Let us recall how we came here: the graces of the first days; the certainty that led us to pronounce the vows; the interior and exterior fecundity with which God has blessed our lives. All these things are signs of a true vocation. On the other hand, if a monk in vows cannot love the Order, and if his whole attitude is destructive and negative, perhaps it might be better that the superiors aid him to obtain a dispensation.

The important thing is that those who do not have a true monastic vocation not make profession. A sincere love of the Order without reservations during the novitiate is a sign of a good vocation. He who later turns against the Order, although before he loved it and showed himself clearly adapted to our life, gives signs of infidelity to his vocation in one way or another.

Stability and Changes in Structures

One result of the process of continual renewal is to move the different monastic Orders toward a closer union. It is evident that there will always be differences between, let us say, the Benedictine life, the Camaldolese life, and the Cistercian life. This variety within the monastic life is very profitable and necessary for the sanctification of the people of God. Within the monastic tradition and even within the Benedictine tradition, there is room for various interpretations. Different accents can produce a variety of approaches which corresponds to the diversity of attractions that the Holy Spirit breathes into souls. But these differences are fewer today thanks, above all, to the search for the authentic function of each institute within the Church.

According to the words of the Council, incorporated now into Church law:

> The principal office of monks is to render to the Divine Majesty a service at once humble and noble within the walls of the monastery, either consecrating themselves entirely, in a retired life, to divine worship, or legitimately undertaking some works of the apostolate or of Christian charity (PC 9).

The legitimacy of these apostolic works depends on their compatibility with the life of solitude and service within the walls of the monastery. It is also governed by the fact that increasingly more works of the apostolate are undertaken by other, better equipped ecclesiastical or civil institutes. The liturgy, for example, is now seen as less of a monastic specialty and more as the heritage of the entire Church (SC 2 and 10).

This deeper consensus concerning the principles of monastic life, especially in its contemplative orientation, will be expressed in all probability by some sort of union, in one single "Monastic Order," of the present monastic Orders. The case of changing from a Cistercian to a Benedictine monastery without having to make a second novitiate can be foreseen. Within this "Monastic Order" there would be, of course, distinct observances and traditions corresponding to the present Orders.

What do such changes imply for the true spirit of our own Order? They imply two things: a pressing need of *authenticity and fidelity* to our vocation, on the one hand; and on the other, what we can call "monastic ecumenism"—an *open attitude*, full of respect and fraternal love toward the other monastic and Benedictine traditions, precisely as "other," that is to say, as different from ours, but authentic and worthwhile on their own grounds. While maintaining the very positive values of this or that spiritual heritage (emphasis on silence, solitude, work, simplicity, or interiority), we should also underline what unites us to other observances (liturgical life, appreciation for prayer, the same Rule, common life, hospitality).

Such a combination of fidelity and openness demands a formation for the monastic life which is relatively complete and, above all, balanced. It implies having clear ideas on what a monk is and on the monastic ideal, as well as on the differences among the various monastic Orders and between these and other religious institutes. Thus we can come to have a true, realistic, and generous love for the Order and for our own community which, for us, is a necessary condition for a life of love centered on Jesus Christ.

Within our own Order or community there can also be changes of structure. What should we do?

It is highly important to know what is of the substance of the monastic life (which is not merely its "spirit") and what is secondary. We shall discuss this difference in more detail in the following chapter. Good monastic formation during the novitiate and the first years of professed life is vital. We must have an adequate understanding of the meaning of our vows, especially of conversion of life. The secondary elements can and will change; the substance of the life does not—the basic observances, a balanced asceticism oriented to prayer, an inner conversion expressed through Benedictine humility.

A monk who is mature and well formed, will know how to do two things at the same time: embrace with enthusiasm the life which he has professed, *as he professed it*, and at the same time keep himself open and flexible for changes that can come in the future. It is inevitable that there be changes. It is a sign of life. The monk must have *confidence in his vocation*, which includes confidence in the action of the Holy Spirit within the Order. God wants the contemplative-monastic life. He positively desires that our communities shine as centers of prayer and contemplative charity. We should live our life in this light.

Stability and Faith

Love of the Order is made concrete in love of the community and the brethren, of *these* brethren, of the brother at my side. Stability depends on this love. Without this living bond of love, stronger than any other, stability of spirit is impossible and corporal stability is made very doubtful and devoid of value.

But in order to have this fraternal love we must live *by faith*. The true spirit of stability depends on a profound faith and on an understanding of the mystery of Divine Providence. Our vocation is the personal expression of God's plan for us. It is our personal way of sharing in the love and wisdom of God which has decreed to save and sanctify men by uniting them within the people of God, under the Head, Christ Jesus.

Therefore my monastery and community are for me a *grace*, a gift from God, and a *mission*, a responsibility. I am responsible for the growth of my brothers and the salvation of many persons. The harmony and perfection of the entire Church depends on my stability in this community. Yes, I might be able to do another work for Christ in another place, but it would not be the work that God has chosen especially for me. Any other work would have less spiritual value, less meaning. Here, even the most insignificant thing is charged with meaning, contributes to God's plan for the union of all of us in Christ, and, therefore is exceptionally pleasing in His eyes.

Much *faith and humility* are necessary to accept one's own situation, one's own monastery with its inevitable human imperfections. Faith and humility are necessary for our pilgrimage in union with our brothers, in the midst of the different modifications of structures and customs demanded by the changes in the modern world. Faith and humility are necessary above all to cover and overcome human deficiencies by a genuine community spirit. Love of the community brings with it the total gift of self to the persons who form that community. Divine redemptive love expresses itself through brotherly love. This is the heart of the vow of stability.

Such love is the central message of the Gospel. If you have this love, your stability and your vocation will never be in danger and you will be able to experience the depths of Christ's joy promised beforehand by the Psalmist: "See how good and pleasant it is, brothers living in unity...Because there God has placed His blessing—eternal life."

For Further Reflection

1. Would you be in favor of modifying the local nature of Benedictine stability, in view of the instability of contemporary society?

2. How have you yourself dealt with the possibility of transferring to another community? What has kept you here?

3. How does the overall principle of monastic asceticism apply to such spiritual values as freedom, creativity, joy, and communication? Why does monastic spirituality seem to stress more apparently passive attitudes, such as humility, fidelity, and silence?

Bibliography

Bernard of Clairvaux, St. *On Precept and Dispensation*, in *The Works of Bernard of Clairvaux I*, Cistercian Fathers Series 1. Spencer: Cistercian Publications, 1970, pp. 103-151.

Braso, G. *Sentier de Vie*, pp. 85-134.

Cunhill, O. in G. Colombas, et al. *San Benito, su vida y su Regla*, pp. 617-619.

Guerric of Igny. *Liturgical Sermons II*. Cistercian Fathers Series 32. Spencer: Cistercian Publications, 1971, pp. 1-8.

McGregor, A. "The Theology of Commitment by Vow", in Region of the Isles, *Symposium on the Vows*, pp. E4-E17.

Peifer, C. *Monastic Spirituality*, pp. 293-302.

Pennington, B., ed. *Contemplative Community, A Symposium*, CS 21, esp. pp. 215-345.

Ratzinger, J. *The Open Circle: The Meaning of Christian Brotherhood*. New York and London: Sheed and Ward, 1966.

Rees, D. et al. *Consider Your Call*, pp. 57-75 and 137-143.

Sortais, G. *Les choses qui plaisent a Dieu*, pp. 199-250.

Steidle, B. *The Rule of St. Benedict*, pp. 54-56 and 287-289.

William of St. Thierry. *The Golden Epistle*. Cistercian Fathers Series 12. Spencer: Cistercian Publications, 1971, pp. 43-45.

Wolter, M. *The Principles of Monasticism*. St. Louis and London: Herder, 1962, pp. 72-87.

CHAPTER SEVEN

SPIRITUALITY AND PROFESSION

An analysis of the five traditional promises of monastic profession, such as that which we have just completed in the foregoing chapters, might seem to suffice for guiding the young monk's formation. All the more so since we have repeatedly stressed the spiritual dimensions of the vows as underlying their more external obligations.

Nevertheless, something is still missing. There is need of a more synthetic approach which would explain the mutual interaction of the vows within the living rhythms of our vocation. We have referred on several occasions to this interaction. The vows form a unity, like steps in the spiritual journey, circling around a central axis. Our growth in this unity requires an appreciation of the axis, which is the spirituality from which the vows flow and to which they are directed. We wish to see the living roots of this spiritual tradition in order to stoop down and drink the water which flows more freely there. This is what the vows are for.

As an aid in this more synthetic approach, the present chapter attempts to explain Benedictine-Cistercian spirituality in terms of the specific spiritual means or methods which characterize it. It is true that there are other, perhaps even more important, elements of monastic spirituality: the Gospel values which it stresses, the life style to which it leads, and the fundamental religious insight by which all the components are oriented to the final purpose of any true Christian spirituality—transformation in Christ. We shall necessarily take a look at these elements, but our attention will be centered on the concrete methods of spirituality which specify the monastic life, since it is these that are most directly related to the vows. They also have special importance for understanding the Rule of Saint Benedict, and we shall use our conclusions to see what profession according to the Rule means.

SPIRITUAL METHODS

Let us first look at these instruments of spirituality in their broader context. For some time now there has been taking place a fruitful encounter between the monasticism of the Western Church and other monastic or contemplative traditions, both Christian and non-Christian. One of the results of this encounter is a sensitivity to "spiritual methods"—systematic ways of proceeding in order to attain personal union with Ultimate Reality. The methods can be either physical or mental, or a mixture of the two. The increased sensitivity to these techniques is chiefly due to the fact that other religious traditions seem to have developed them more explicitly than has the Benedictine-Cistercian school.

There have been different reactions to this situation on the part of western monasticism. The first result was to incorporate, in one way or another, certain methods of asceticism and prayer which have proved fruitful for other traditions. A second approach, sometimes combined with the first one, has been to emphasize monastic hospitality as the particular contribution which western monasteries have to offer at the present time.

A third attitude, not necessarily opposed to the other two, consists in reexamining the western tradition in order to see if we have not neglected, in theory or in practice, spiritual methods which do in fact exist in it. This approach coincides with our desire to enter more deeply into Benedictine spirituality. It can also be of considerable help to us in understanding the spirit of the vows, since the latter are fundamentally nothing else than methods which the Christian spiritual tradition has found to be especially useful in man's paschal pilgrimage with Christ to the Father. Such a clarification would also seem to be a prerequisite for the healthy incorporation of elements from other monastic currents, for the spiritual benefit of all concerned.

In this chapter, then, we shall indicate the broad lines of such a reexamination. Our way of procedure will be first inductive and historical, then deductive and explanatory, with special reference to the numerous relations between spiritual methods and monastic profession.

1. POLITEIA AND CONVERSATIO

The primacy of conversion of life, *conversatio morum*, among the different elements of monastic profession should be evident by now. In fact, monastic conversion, if properly understood, not only gives a fundamental orientation to the other elements of our life, but also sums them all up in a unified "manner of life," the literal translation of *conversatio*. We have seen this at length in Chapter Two.

Not so evident, however, is the fact that Benedictine *conversatio* has its historical roots in the spiritual methods of the Desert Fathers as expressed by the Greek word *politeia*. In classical Greek culture this term signified the political constitution or regime of a city-state, especially the relation of the citizen to the body politic. Even prior to the Desert Fathers, however, it was used by writers to indicate a personal manner of behavior, a way of life. Whereas the word *bios* referred to the more exterior and historically conditioned aspects of one's life, and *zoe* to sentient life, *politeia* signified the life of virtue, the moral life with the means which are chosen to achieve it and to express it. In this sense it could be translated as "ascetic life style."

A highly significant example of this more spiritual meaning is Saint Paul's use of *politeia* in Eph. 2:12, and Phil. 1:27 and 3:20, where it is translated in the Latin Vulgate as *conversatio*. The two words, however, are not entirely equivalent since *conversatio* was also used to translate other words, especially *anastrophe*—"good conduct." Modern translations of *politeia* vary considerably: citizenship, homeland, community, membership, conduct, everyday life. But the general sense is clear. Membership in a social group implies a new way of life to be practiced and interiorized by the member.

In primitive monasticism, the driving force behind its development was the search for the best *politeia*, the most efficacious ascetic practice. The first monks were convinced of the need of concrete practices as spiritual methods to purify the soul, to pass from vice to virtue and from virtue to God. Each monk or group of monks had his *politeia*, his particular rule of life, the observances which he would cultivate over a certain period of time, for example, a year, in order to grow in self-denial and liberty of spirit.

Obviously they sometimes went to extremes in matters such as fasting, sitting on a column, using chains, or not looking at anyone. At times these ascetic methods became occasions more of pride than of stability, solitude, silence, or true self-denial. Yet perhaps such things were necessary for them. Our modern tendency may lie in the opposite direction, a hidden mistrust of concrete observances. One of the effects of a good monastic formation will be a balanced view on this whole matter of observances and life style, since it constitutes one of the characteristic features of our tradition.

The need for a definite rule of life as a method of spiritual combat is reflected in most of the sayings of the Desert Fathers, especially in their replies to the question, "What should I do to be saved?" We have already seen some examples of this in Chapter Two. Here are three more sayings, simply as illustrations:

A brother asked Abba Arsenius for a saving word. The elder replied: Fight with all your strength to have your interior life pleasing to God. If you do this you will also overcome your bodily passions.

Abba Anthony said: Keep the fear of God always before your eyes. Remember Him who takes life away and gives it back. Hate the world and all worldliness. Flee from comforts. Renounce the present life and live in God alone. Remember what you have promised to God since that is what He will ask from you on Judgment Day. Bear with hunger, thirst, and naked-ness. Keep vigil, repent, weep, and groan in your hearts. Despise the flesh so as to save your souls.

Abba Pastor said: Get away from any man who always argues every time he talks.

In cenobitic circles the charism of the organizers of the common life, such as Saint Pachomius, was to establish a *politeia* suitable for a large number of men. It was "common" in the double sense of the word— relatively uniform and relatively normal, suitable for the "common man." John Cassian describes such a life style in considerable detail in his *Institutes*, using the Latin term *conversatio*. In fact the immediate purpose of the many monastic rules written through the ages is to ensure the authenticity of the community's *politeia, conversatio*, or ascetic way of life. These rules, prior to being legal codes, are selections, systematizations and applications of spiritual methods which have been proven by experience to be effective for spiritual growth. An institu-tional framework is not necessarily alien to these methods, provided it is used with spiritual understanding. Indeed, common life, from which the institution grows, is itself an excellent spiritual technique.

For Saint Benedict, in particular, the whole life which he outlines and legislates for in his Rule is the monk's *conversatio*, his chosen way of spiritual growth, by which he hopes to purify his heart in dependence on Christ "and thus merit to accompany Him in His kingdom" (RB Prol., 50). The content of the monk's *conversatio* is, then, a specific spiritual way incorporating different methods which experience has shown to be helpful for growth in Christ.

We can draw two important conclusions from this brief historical sketch. In the first place, the monk is one who assumes an ascetic program of life as his particular spiritual way on the return journey to his Creator. The following section will study this in more detail. In the second place, this program of life is the specific meaning of the Rule of Saint Benedict. The last part of this chapter will clarify what is implied for monastic profession by such an interpretation of the Rule. We can already see, however, that the monk's commitment should be under-stood and lived within this larger spiritual context.

2. A TRIPLE WAY

Reflecting on the lived experience of those men and women who have embraced the way of life sketched by Saint Benedict, we begin to see that at the heart of Benedictine-Cistercian spirituality there exists a complete and coherent way of spiritual growth. It represents the fruit of many centuries of experience prior to and following the writing of the RB. According to this hypothesis we are dealing with a whole program of life directly centered on Christ, incorporating in itself three spiritual methods which are based on the inner structure of human existence and which interact dynamically among themselves in the life of the monk. These three methods are:

-monastic observance
-*lectio divina*
-Benedictine humility

In this section we shall first see how this spiritual way is expressed in the RB. Then we can examine its principal implications and its more practical consequences in the life of the vows.

Spiritual Art

Saint Benedict calls his general program of monastic conversion an art, *ars spiritalis*, "spiritual art," or better, "the art of growth in the spirit" (RB 4, 75). The context of this phrase shows that it refers to the entire life program "practiced unceasingly day and night...within the monastic enclosure" (RB 4, 76-78). The Latin word *ars* corresponds to the Greek *techne*, an applied science. This indicates the background of the Rule's references to the monk as a workman or technician skilled in this spiritual craft, the craft of monastic *conversatio* (RB Prol., 14 and 7, 70).

In his chapter on "the instruments of the spiritual art" (RB 4, 75), Saint Benedict lumps together many seemingly heterogeneous elements of spiritual method. These include not only the general Christian virtues, but also corporal practices, with the mental discipline and the dispositions of spirit necessary for these observances to have their intended effect. Literary analysis has shown that a particular preoccupation of Benedict in this list of instruments was to add specifically monastic techniques to a previously existing compilation which seems to have been inspired by a more general lay spirituality.

This preoccupation is based on the relation between these instruments of the spiritual art and the *politeia*, or ascetic methods of the Desert Fathers. The relation can be seen in comparing a practice such as that given in RB 4, 73 ("Make peace before nightfall with a person with whom there has been some disagreement") with the following apothegm of the Fathers:

> Abba Epiphanius invited Abba Hilarion for a meal and offered him some chicken. The latter, however, refused to eat it, saying that from the day he received the monastic habit he had never eaten meat. Abba Epiphanius

replied: "For my part, I have never gone to sleep at night without first making peace with the brothers with whom I have had some disagreement during the day." Abba Hilarion admitted: "Your *politeia* is better than mine."

It is true that there may not be any direct literary dependence between this incident and the text of the Rule, since both could depend on Eph. 4:26, but the similarity of literary style and spiritual message is obvious. The relation is also apparent in the vocabulary used by Abba Pastor and taken up by Saint Benedict:

> Abba Pastor said: To prostrate oneself in the presence of God, to overcome pride and reject self-will, these are the instruments by which the soul accomplishes its work.

In the twelfth century the various instruments of the spiritual art were known as "exercises" or "disciplines," and a distinction was made between those which were more corporal (exterior observances) and those more spiritual (reading, meditation, prayer, and contemplation). Modern commentators on the Rule have stressed the Divine Office, interior prayer, stability, separation from the world, the steps of humility, and the cenobitic life itself, as fundamental methods in Benedictine spirituality.

Saint Benedict himself does not systematize his spiritual art in a manner which would satisfy modern man's desire for a secure and clear-cut spiritual method. The closest he comes to this is in the degrees of humility, with their three basic elements of obedience, interior humiliation, and silence as steps in the pilgrimage from fear of the Lord to perfect charity (RB 7). Commentators have rightly stressed the importance of these steps of humility in the spiritual life, but their place within the overall program of Benedictine life has not been clear. What is their relation to the corporal discipline of observances and to the spiritual discipline of lectio divina? This is not a new question. It is basically the same point which was at issue in the controversies between the first Cistercians and the monks of Cluny in the twelfth century, as well as in similar discussions at the time of the reform at La Trappe in the seventeenth century.

To answer this question it seems best to say that there are three different and complementary types of spiritual disciplines operating within the life described by Saint Benedict: humility of heart as sketched in Chapters 5-7 and 71-72; the traditional monastic observances as laid down throughout the Rule; and *lectio divina*, with *meditatio* and *oratio* leading to *contemplatio*, as developed in later monastic experience and writings. The other ascetic techniques in Benedictine-Cistercian spirituality seem to be included in these three general methods which, when taken together, form the Benedictine *conversatio*.

These three general methods constitute the second of three levels of spiritual discipline in Benedictine life: the overall program or way of life (*conversatio*); the three general methods of spirituality which specify this way of life, as indicated above; and the concrete techniques or elements (*instrumenta*) of which the three more general methods are composed. For the sake of clarity, we restrict the use of the word "method" in the rest of this book to the three more general exercises with which we are directly concerned.

It should also be pointed out that faith, hope, and charity, as theological virtues, and prudence, discernment, or "discretion, the mother of the virtues" (RB 64, 19), as well as Baptism and the other Sacraments, are not strictly speaking parts of spiritual methods but rather their guiding principles. Spiritual methods flow from them rather than vice versa. A Christian monk knows that true spiritual growth is a gift, a grace which "the Spirit breathes where He wills" (Jn. 3:8). Any form of asceticism is merely a more or less necessary way of removing obstacles to this grace, preparing the different dimensions of man to receive the Lord, and expressing the gifts already received. Moreover, methods are not custom-made. They have to be fitted to the grace and growth of each person. They are made for man, not man for them. These principles of faith must be kept clearly in view as we live the spiritual methods which are a necessary part of our profession.

Doctrinal Context

While distinguishing three general disciplines within Benedictine-Cistercian asceticism, we must be careful, as I mentioned above, not to project onto the author of the Rule a systematic mentality which is more of the twentieth century than of the sixth. Saint Benedict was not a theoretician, but a spiritual father and legislator with a unique gift for synthesizing different strands of the Christian monastic tradition into a liveable whole. Nevertheless, there are two important factors which have intervened to prevent a clearer appreciation of his *conversatio*. These impediments are interrelated: the lack within western spirituality of a consistent vision of human existence, and a tendency to emphasize extrinsic law and order rather than intrinsic value and growth. For a more adequate understanding, therefore, of the methods of Benedictine spirituality, it will be helpful first to see their anthropological context and then to point out their meaning as aspects of the Christian mystery.

Man's Total Development

Actually, there does exist in monastic tradition a certain anthropology, or vision of man, which has led to a common mode of expressing the art of spiritual growth. This vision results from monasticism's interest in *the whole man*.

Man is seen as totally dependent on the Word of God addressed to him in Christ Jesus. The Word reverberates in the different parts of his being. True human growth is a process of increasing purification and unification of man's total being by this Word. As we saw in the dynamics of Christian chastity, the different levels of human existence must all be assumed and recentered under Christ the Head, so that man may transcend himself in increasing transparency of the body to the soul and of the soul to truth and to love. This process of integration and interpenetration has been called by different names: "divinization" in the Eastern tradition, "transformation" more commonly in the West, "unity of love" by Cassian (Conf. 10, 7), "the heights of doctrine and virtue" by Saint Benedict (RB 73, 9), "unity of spirit" by the Cistercians of the twelfth century.

If we ask how monastic writers express their vision of the whole man, we frequently find them using a threefold description of human existence, corresponding to the trilogy of *body*, *soul*, and *spirit* which Saint Paul applies to Christian life in his first canonical letter (I Thess. 5:23). Origen in the third century did not hesitate to use equivalent terms to explain both his doctrine of spiritual combat and the meanings of Sacred Scripture, though his vocabulary, like Paul's, is not always consistent. The three dimensions of man have been implicit in Christian spirituality since Origen's time, although some more speculative writers have occasionally abused them by not sufficiently distinguishing man's nature from God's grace, thus minimizing the gratuitous nature of true spiritual experience. The trilogy, however, is at the basis of the formulation by Evagrius Ponticus in the fourth century, underlies Cassian's teachings in the fifth (Conf. 3, 6-10 and 4, 18-21), and thus forms the general view of man which serves as a background for the spiritual program offered by the RB in the sixth century.

Saint Benedict refers to these three elements in one of the fundamental texts of the Rule. There, he points to a transcendent reality in each one of us, an inner thrust related to humility of heart, which connects, as it were, and gives direction to both body and soul:

The ladder thus raised up is our life here below, which the Lord raises up to heaven by humbling our heart. The sides of this ladder are our body and soul. Into these sides our divine calling has set the different steps of humility and discipline which we must climb (RB 7, 8-9).

In the centuries after Saint Benedict, it was William of St. Thierry, writing in the twelfth century, who best crystallized and formulated this anthropology, creatively using the intuitions of Origen, Gregory of Nyssa, and Saint Augustine. William did this especially in his chief work, the *Golden Epistle*, in which he sums up his spiritual teaching. Here is an example:

> It is because he has become one spirit with God that a person is spiritual. This is the perfection of man in this life. Hitherto solitary or alone, he now becomes united and his solitude of body is changed into unity of spirit. Our Lord's prayer for his disciples, summing up the whole of perfection, is fulfilled in him: "Father, my will is that as I and you are one, so they too may be one in us." This unity of man with God, or likeness to God, brings the soul, which is inferior to the spirit, into conformity with it to the degree in which the spirit draws near to God. In the same way, the body, which is inferior to the soul, becomes like the latter. Thus the spirit, the soul, and the body are duly set in order and established in their proper place, rightly appreciated and even thought about in accordance with their particular characteristics. So man begins to know himself perfectly, advance through this self-knowledge, and grow in the knowledge of God (nn. 287-289).

Saint Bernard of Clairvaux, who was a close friend of William, can help us understand the meaning of these different dimensions of human life. Although Bernard tends to avoid the use of special terms to indicate a "place" in man's soul where God is experienced, nevertheless he points out a strong moral duality in man's use or abuse of his spiritual powers.

Bernard centers his vision of man on the use of free will. The resulting dynamism of his spirituality implies a moral world view rather than an ontological or static one. Rather it is a fusion of the two approaches. Thus within the usual body-soul division he stresses a deeper duality in the soul itself—that of *freedom from constraint* (free will) which can become "self-will" and lead man into an egoistical region of unlikeness to God, and a *freedom from sin* which springs from "common will," in which likeness to God is found. It is at this "point," that is, through this inner relation of united wills, that purified love empties the soul of sin and of the illusory personality of self-will in order to inebriate man, taking him out of himself in unity of spirit with God. We shall see below how Bernard, following Saint Benedict, describes the role of humility in this liberation from inner falsehood.

In recent centuries greater precision has been given to this duality of man's spiritual powers and to the resulting threefold description of human existence. Thus Saint John of the Cross refers to the "substance of the soul," distinct from both its sensory part and its spiritual faculties (intellect, will, and memory). It is the soul's "deepest center" which, he explains, is attainable through love (*Living Flame*, I, 9).

In our own times, Thomas Merton and others have followed Saint Bernard's doctrine of a false self, but have developed at greater length its positive counterpart. Merton's essential contribution to monastic spirituality will probably be seen to have been the incorporation of the messages of existential personalism, modern psychology, and non-Christian mysticism into the mainstream of western monastic life. This living integration is achieved through the common denominator of "identity," "our true self, in the divine image" (*The New Man*, 73-77), as the necessary path to union with God.

Accordingly, the monk is a person who is continually in search of God and who, as a necessary part of this search, endeavors through an inner transformation to attain to an ever deeper consciousness of his true self in the presence of the risen Christ. This objective is very similar to what Cassian and Saint Benedict implied in their concept of "purity of heart," the inner serenity which we have already seen as a key to the spirit of our vow of conversion. It is also very close to what Saint Bernard meant by "common will": man's total surrender to God and to his brothers, not only by an external form of obedience, but also by a renunciation of all false self-images. There is a treasure hidden and attainable within the body-soul composite, calling man to go beyond himself. This is achieved through humility and through love, as we shall see below.

There is obviously much room for further experience and reflection on the meaning of the terms *body*, *soul* (*mind*), and *spirit* (*heart*), with a needed study of their use by different writers. But our short survey of monastic authors shows the solid tradition of a trilogy of dimensions in man and the application of monastic disciplines to these three dimensions. The trilogy is presented in terms of the transcendent vocation (*evocatio divina*, RB 7, 9) of the human person and can only be understood in terms of ongoing spiritual growth, not as a description of a static essence. Understood correctly, it is neither unorthodox nor incompatible with the classic body-soul distinction, but rather explains in terms of spiritual maturity what the body-soul terminology leaves unsaid.

Body, in this sense, is not only the skeleton with its muscles and organs, but more directly implies man's living emotional make-up, his temperament, affectivity, and unconscious elements. *Soul*, or *mind*, refers to the conscious activity of the intellect, will, and memory: discursive reasoning, intuitive understanding, abiding attitudes which govern the more external acts of the body. It is related to the *ego* of modern psychology.

It is more difficult, if not impossible, to name adequately man's most inner yet transcendent dimension, since the word *spirit* has different connotations in different languages and cultures. The reality is based, however, on the fact that man's rational activities do not exhaust his spiritual capacities. Beyond or underneath his discursive and intuitive powers, there exists an inner meeting place of truth and love, being and action, ontology and morality. It is primarily a *receptive capacity* for transcendental life and has been called for this reason an "obediential potency" (ST III, 11, 1). It is an openness to be wounded and to give oneself totally both to God and to men in a fundamental option of redemptive love. The average nun or monk probably experiences it in an indirect manner as an inner, somewhat illusive, yet deeply vital and satisfying relational center of silent recollection, prayer, and inspiration. There you are present to the Presence.

Secondarily, this dimension is an *operative capacity* at the root of both body and soul which can orient and unite all human powers and which thus expresses itself through them. Both as receptive and as operative, it is frequently referred to as the *heart*, as in Cassian (Conf. 14, 10) and RB. It is also called *conscience* (*conscientia*), whether in medieval literature (RB 7, 35 and the *Sermons* of Saint Bernard) or more recently, as in the Pastoral Constitution of Vatican II on the Church in the Modern World:

> Conscience is the most secret core and sanctuary of a man. There he is alone with God, whose voice echoes in his inmost being. In a wonderful manner conscience reveals that law which is fulfilled by love of God and neighbor. In fidelity to conscience, Christians are joined with the rest of men in their search for truth (GS 16).

This inner nucleus of the personality is man's true self, his spiritual center of gravity. It is the central meeting ground of his being, from which both body and soul spring forth, like "sides of a ladder" (RB 7, 9), as interlocked expressions of an inner reality in which they meet in a flame of openness to the Spirit of God.

Cassian and Benedict are following biblical language when they call this deepest integrating principle the *heart*. According to the consistent teaching of Sacred Scripture, it is the central originating point of man's affections and knowledge. From it "the mouth speaks" and each man shows what he is (Mt. 12:34-35). Saint Paul uses both *heart* and *spirit* to indicate this most precious of human realities, probably in order to bring out the heart's receptive connaturality with the Spirit of God

(Rom. 5:5 and 8:5-16). Christ wishes to live here by faith (Eph. 3:17) and it is here that the monk can find his true identity as a son in the Son, according as the Spirit witnesses to his spirit.

The writers mentioned above usually refer to the three dimensions of man in relation to different stages of the spiritual journey. Our concern here, however, is not so much with the chronological sequence of the distinct periods of growth, as with the *underlying spiritual methods which are present throughout the process*, though in varying degrees. It is a question of the interrelated procedures by which a person may pass—or dispose himself to pass—from self-love to the perfection of oblative love and thus to the experience of Ultimate Reality, since "God is love" (I Jn. 4:8).

We are now in a position to understand these procedures more clearly, having seen the tridimensional nature of man which forms the river bed, as it were, of Benedictine life. Thus we can distinguish within the general program offered by Benedictine-Cistercian spirituality these three exercises or methods of spiritual growth, with their respective relations to the three levels of human existence:

-*Monastic observances* integrate man's bodily dimension.

-*Lectio divina* integrates man's intellectual activity.

-*Humility of heart* integrates man's spirit and disposes the whole man for unity with God's Spirit.

Diagram II attempts to present synthetically these three dimensions of the Benedictine spiritual art with their respective components, showing something of their interrelation and finality. The five traditional vows of profession, marked here with asterisks, can be seen in their proper context of *conversatio*, and with their respective functions at the service of the whole man made anew in the image of Christ.

A DIVINE MILIEU

From this diagram we can see how the different methods offered by Benedictine spirituality are based not only on a vision of the whole man, but even more on the monk's living insertion into the reality of Christ. They seem to reflect other threefold expressions of Christian life, although we should avoid overstressing the parallels since we are dealing with spiritual realities, not with mathematics. Nevertheless, the general methods of *exercitia corporalia*, *lectio*, and *humilitas* seem to be, in the first place, particular ways by which the monk shares in the threefold activity of the Savior, as King, Prophet, and Priest

Diagram II

METHODS IN BENEDICTINE SPIRITUALITY

The elements or instruments of this spiritual art constitute three general methods of growth in the Spirit, according to the fundamental expressions of man's personality. They are to be used "with prudence and charity" (RB 64, 14) so that their objective (purity of heart) and their end (eternal life or transformation in Christ) may be achieved.

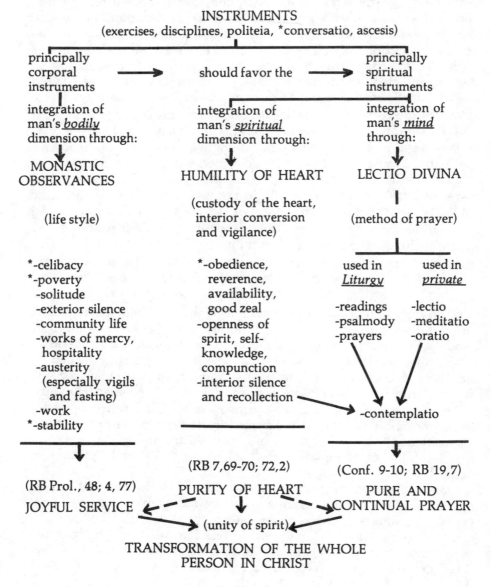

INSTRUMENTS
(exercises, disciplines, politeia, *conversatio, ascesis)

principally corporal instruments → should favor the → principally spiritual instruments

integration of man's _bodily_ dimension through: | integration of man's _spiritual_ dimension through: | integration of man's _mind_ through:

MONASTIC OBSERVANCES | HUMILITY OF HEART | LECTIO DIVINA

(life style) | (custody of the heart, interior conversion and vigilance) | (method of prayer)

*-celibacy
*-poverty
-solitude
-exterior silence
-community life
-works of mercy, hospitality
-austerity (especially vigils and fasting)
-work
*-stability

*-obedience, reverence, availability, good zeal
-openness of spirit, self-knowledge, compunction
-interior silence and recollection

used in _Liturgy_ | used in _private_

-readings
-psalmody
-prayers

-lectio
-meditatio
-oratio

-contemplatio

(RB 7,69-70; 72,2)

(RB Prol., 48; 4, 77)
JOYFUL SERVICE

PURITY OF HEART

(Conf. 9-10; RB 19,7)
PURE AND CONTINUAL PRAYER

(unity of spirit)

TRANSFORMATION OF THE WHOLE
PERSON IN CHRIST

(cf. LG 10-13). Saint Benedict appears to have sensed this participation when he urges us "to battle under the Lord Christ, the true King,...to listen with attentive ears to His divine voice...as He shows us the way to His holy tent by saying: He dwells here who walks without fault, acts with justice, and speaks truth from his heart" (RB Prol., 3, 9, 24-26).

In more general terms, these disciplines constitute a triple spiritual way which is neither automatic nor short in duration, but which respects both the deepest rhythms of human life, as we saw in the preceding section, as well as the Lordship of Christ, who alone, by his Spirit, can achieve man's divine vocation. In fact the disciplines correspond closely to these two poles of orientation: man open to God and God who saves man. They serve as a sort of coupling device between the two by expressing the inner demands of faith, hope, and charity on the practical level of daily living. They thus heal the divisions caused by sin both within or among men, and between man and God. In the same way, they foster a new personal and communal transparency to the divine Persons—trusting fidelity in the Father's promises expands into increasing sensitivity to the divine Word, and bears fruit in deeper dependence on the action of the Holy Spirit.

A prime example of these divine and human dimensions of the monk's Christian experience is found in the Blessed Virgin Mary. Her total confidence in God's action meant that her virginal body was completely submissive to the plan of the Father. Her soul (*psyche*), which had magnified the Lord, was pierced through by the sword of God's Word so that out of the hearts of many men, her spiritual children, thoughts might be revealed. And her spirit (*pneuma*) rejoiced in God's saving mercy toward her humble condition (cf. Lk. 1:34-2:35). These three levels of Mary's spiritual experience are closely related to her three graces of virginity, fecundity, and humility, as sung by Saint Bernard in his sermons *On the Glories of the Virgin Mother*. Humility of heart appears in this light as a primary expression of her Immaculate Conception. Vatican II links them in its description of her inner dispositions: "With a full heart and impeded by no sin, she devoted herself totally as a handmaid of the Lord to the person and work of her Son" (LG 56).

Mary's fullness of grace has a special importance for the monk. The monastic calling implies creating an atmosphere which expresses and promotes a similar openness to the Father, the Word, and the Spirit. It is meant to be a divine milieu, both exterior to us, through monastic observances, and interior, through *lectio* and especially humility. These three disciplines are, in fact, the basic structures of Benedictine life.

Within this general atmosphere of total devotion to Christ there is room for considerable liberty of spirit. Benedictine-Cistercian spirituality, contrary to most eastern monastic traditions, puts emphasis more on general life style than on detailed bodily or mental disciplines. This is due to the importance of a deeply personal response to the Word. Nevertheless, when it is a question of transforming the whole man, everything hangs together. As with Christian asceticism in general, the different aspects of monastic life seem to be mutually necessary. Experience teaches that when one or another of its elements is either excessively neglected or excessively stressed, the whole process of growth suffers. In fact, the various movements and reforms within monastic spirituality through the centuries have had for their purpose the reestablishment of a healthy balance among the different elements. This balance, the famous "Benedictine equilibrium," is not an end in itself, but a means for total personal integration and a more complete experience of God. Thus it is important to understand the purpose of the three interacting methods. The following is a brief resume of their main points in the light of the principles which we have just seen.

Monastic Observance

There are many possible ways of enumerating the basic *exercitia corporalia*, which are the elements of the Benedictine-Cistercian life style. In preceding chapters we have grouped them according to their relations with the vows of profession, especially that of conversion. For the sake of simplicity they have sometimes been reduced to the three "L"s—liturgy, labor, and *lectio*—as the three pivotal points of the Benedictine horarium. Liturgy (*Opus Dei*) and *lectio* would be taken, in this case, in their external aspect of observances, rather than as an interiorized method of prayer. But other elements such as solitude, fasting, and vigils must evidently be included, not to mention poverty, chastity, and stability, which have been raised to the level of vows. It is important to see that these are the fundamental corporal disciplines of monastic life, not the details of a code of prescriptions, customs, or local usages. They are those observances, and only those, without which the life style would not be conducive to the transformation for which Benedictine or Cistercian life attempts to prepare.

As we saw in Chapter Two, the common life, though containing in itself a special mystery of Christ's presence (Mt. 18:20), is also a discipline, and a very important one. It should give a cenobitic tonality of dialogue, friendship, fraternal mercy, compenetration, and celebration to the entire complex of prayer, humility, and ascetic practices. Similarly, hospitality and the other corporal works of mercy (RB 4, 14-19; 36, 1; 53, 1) have special spiritual overtones, though they, too, must be integrated into the broader horizon of Benedictine or Cistercian spirituality. The inner attitude which is the source of this fraternal charity is called "good zeal" in RB 72. Its interior quality makes it a component of humility of heart, as we shall see below.

One of the important fruits of contemporary monastic renewal is to show the intrinsic value of the basic ascetic observances, as opposed to an emphasis on their mere physical strictness or their material conformity to this or that piece of monastic legislation. Thus there takes place a passage from a spirituality of external forms to one of lived values. As a means to this, the Christian meaning of each of the elements should be understood. Taken together, as a general spiritual method, their direct purpose is to express on the level of the body the constellation of Gospel values that are fostered by the monastic vocation, according to the general principle of sacramentality and the Incarnation. In the process they become an external imitation and extension of the historical life of Christ. Looking more to the future, they anticipate the subordination of all creation to the kingdom of the Father (I Cor. 15:24-28). They thus become, in a special way, manifestations of Christian hope.

The need for a balance among these corporal disciplines is sometimes overlooked or not sufficiently appreciated. On the one hand, the different monastic activities produce a peaceful and healthy rhythm for human growth. They even help develop hidden talents. However, as we saw in the previous chapter, sooner or later experience shows another aspect—there is a type of human frustration built into this famous "monastic peace"! No one single activity taken individually, such as work, sacred art, study, or even personal prayer, is allowed full scope for a development which other, more specialized life styles might permit. This built-in frustration, which usually affects us precisely where we are most personally sensitive, often passes unnoticed to the casual observer. But it has important spiritual repercussions. It forces us to transcend the merely human dimension of our daily activities and base our life more exclusively on theological faith and hope. The equilibrium of monastic discipline can thus provoke a real inner enlightenment based on personal experience. We learn that the Christian meaning of the observances, as outlined in the preceding paragraph, is the only one which ultimately satisfies the human heart and gives "the peace which the world cannot give" (Jn. 14:27).

It is chiefly on the level of these corporal exercises that Benedictine spiritual art can integrate certain practices of Yoga and Zen Buddhism.

This, however, brings up the very interesting question of the relation of these and all monastic observances to the unconscious elements of the human psyche. Yoga exercises, for example, seem to be based directly on the inner order of the psyche which, however, may not be the same for Westerners as for Asiatics. Without developing this point here, we should recognize it as a vital aspect of the corporal observances. It can provide a renewed appreciation for these fundamental bodily disciplines which make up what Cassian called "the first renunciation" (Conf. 3, 6-7). They constitute the first general spiritual method which Benedictine monasticism has to offer. Since they reflect the principle of visible embodiment of spiritual realities, which is at the heart of monastic spirituality, these disciplines are what most distinguish the monk's life from other forms of Christian living. The exterior commitments of profession coincide with this dimension.

Lectio Divina

The second general method is *lectio divina*. This is important as constituting the traditional monastic pedagogy of prayer. We have given a brief description of it in Chapter Two. The explication of the sequence, *lectio-meditatio-oratio-contemplatio*, occurred in the centuries which followed upon Saint Benedict, although each of these four elements is referred to in the Rule. This gradual elaboration was a good example of the general phenomenon of development from an implicit method, a repeated pattern of human acts aimed at some goal, to an explicit one, a systematized way of procedure. *Lectio* is what usually happens when you listen sincerely to the Word.

According to this prayer method, the Christian, created and called by the Word of God, passes from hearing or reading this Word to its active assimilation. For this he uses his imagination and discursive faculties, but above all a vocal or merely mental repetition of a word or phrase (*ruminatio*). This form of simple meditation passes almost naturally into a more direct, intimate, and personal encounter with God: *oratio*. It becomes one's *own* prayer, the spontaneous expression of one's deepest convictions and feelings.

Whereas *oratio* is the overflow of the heart into the discursive faculties, *contemplatio* implies a certain submerging of these faculties deep into the heart. It is a gratuitous gift from the Lord, a form of the *excessus*, or total surrender, to which Saint Bernard refers in describing the passage from self-love to divine love. This temporary loss of self-dominion for the sake of unification presupposes and activates the third, contemplative renunciation described by Cassian in Conf. 3, 6-7. We have already seen it in Chapter Two.

Peaceful rumination of an inspired word or phrase seems to dispose you for *contemplatio* more than does a discursive meditation. The latter usually tends toward one or another form of *oratio*. As Cassian (Conf. 9, 2-8; 10, 6-14) frequently points out, growth in prayer and contemplation is a clear example of how the different dimensions of man's being, with their respective spiritual disciplines, interact in mutual aid or hindrance.

Nevertheless, the Lord, who is Spirit, comes and goes as He wants. The total gift of self, which is implied in the *excessus* of contemplation, is itself a pure gift of divine love. That is why a prolonged, somewhat dry and even disagreeable prayer of deep desire is often a key factor in monastic lectio.

This fourfold method of prayer also forms the basis of the community's liturgical prayer. It constitutes, as well, the underlying rhythm of most supplementary methods of personal prayer, such as shared prayer, the "Jesus prayer," centering prayer, or transcendental meditation. It seems to reflect the fundamental structure of the human person in his gradual interiorization of truth, from sense knowledge to total spiritual commitment. Thus the Christian monk, through meditative reading and prayer, retraces the path by which the Word of God reaches him. He passes through the meanings of the written, spoken, and lived Word in order to relive salvation history in himself and arrive at the same personal experience of Christ's saving Sonship in the light of which the Scriptures were written.

This inner movement toward Christ, which makes explicit the very substance of Christian faith, is the typical feature of Benedictine prayer. In the past it has protected monastic lectio from being just another external observance. It seems to be especially important today in preventing contemplation from turning into a mere psychological game. Insofar as lectio establishes this abiding attitude of living faith, it is an essential part of the spirit of the vows.

Humility

Chapters 7 and 72 are rightly considered to be the heart of the Rule. What is there called *humilitas* is the chief method which Benedictine life offers as a way to God. It constitutes the basic factor in the spirit and practice of the vows and is the core of Benedictine-Cistercian spirituality. The transcendent nature of the spirit, or heart, which we have noted in the trilogy, body, soul, and spirit, explains why Benedictine humility is the reality governing both corporal expressions and the life of prayer. It is to the heart that the Master speaks (RB Prol., 1) and from the heart that the sweetness of charity and the purity of prayer spring forth (RB Prol., 49 and 20, 3-4). The spiritual life is essentially the life of a heart created anew by the grace of the risen Christ.

Thus the fundamental element and purpose of the monk's life is not essentially different from that of any Christian. On the contrary, by discovering the interior attractions and instincts written by grace in your inner heart, you touch the Heart of Christ, you become capable of reaching the inner heart of your brothers in community and of vibrating with the truest desires of all men. It is above all a question of letting these deepest instincts toward truth and sacrificial love, that are secretly present and active in you, take ever greater possession of your whole being. Thoughts, desires, will, and feelings have to come into harmony with the inner action of the Spirit, have to be integrated at the center of your being, your heart. This is the spiritual virginity which we saw as the inner meaning of chastity. All growth in the spiritual life could be defined as a "return to the heart."

It is humility that guides us in this return journey, that uncovers the false instincts in the human heart and finds the truth written there by grace. This is the true self which the Greek text of I Peter 3:4 describes as "the hidden man of the heart whose unfading beauty is a meek and quiet spirit, precious in God's eyes."

This makes it easier to understand how Benedict's concept of humility closely resembles that of biblical conversion, *metanoia*—a change of mentality that includes ideas and concepts but goes beyond them to touch the very roots of man's existence. The steps of humility and good zeal are really degrees of conversion of heart, as expressed in the realities of cenobitic obedience, self-knowledge, and silence.

Perhaps this *humilitas* is best summed up in the phrase, *tacite conscientia patientiam amplectatur*, "the monk embraces patience silently in his inner heart" (RB 7, 35). What is described here is a disciplined and thoroughly humble spirit of union with the silent Christ in His passion and resurrection. More than any other phrase in the Rule, this one shows the essential connection between humble good zeal and an interior dimension of the human spirit that embraces in love what the exterior senses and the discursive faculties judge to be folly. It shows, too, how the very limitations and defects of one's community form part of the Benedictine spiritual method, for him who has ears to hear. Such a truly converted conscience, Cassian's "purity of heart" (Conf. 1, 4-11), is the precious fruit of a life of real self-renunciation.

Saint Bernard of Clairvaux clarified and developed the dynamics of Benedictine humility as a way to the true self. His treatise on *The Steps of Humility and Pride*, a typically Bernardine elaboration of Saint Benedict's *humilitas*, shows how humility is a return to truth—truth in one's self, in one's neighbor, in God. Since Christ Himself is the Truth, He is also the way of humility and has led us in this way by His own experience of infinite self-emptying and compassion. We follow Him in this road of meekness, first of all, by passing judgment on ourselves and admitting that, despite all our labors, we are useless servants (RB 7, 49). This initial knowledge of our true self teaches us how much we depend on God's overwhelming mercy and how much our brother, too, is an object of this mercy. These two truths—my own complete dependence on the mercy of God and your similar dependence—act as pincers to extract the blinding bar of pride from the eye of the heart. This lets us contemplate Truth in Itself, which is deeper even than the ground of our being. It is thus that we recognize and overcome our false self, with its steps of pride: curiosity, thoughtlessness, silly mirth, boasting, and the like, which Bernard describes with zest and satirical humor.

The inner paradox of humility is the paradox of the Gospel itself: loss and gain of self, death and resurrection, the last shall be first. It is not merely a psychic movement, but above all a theological one. The Spirit of God centers both the soul and the body on Christ. Jesus asks us to enter into ourselves not so much by *introspection* as by *compunction*. The difference is important. The inward movement of humility is not so much a matter of hiding ourselves within ourselves, as a liberation of ourselves, which takes place in the depths of our being, and lets us *out* of ourselves from the inside by a surrender to Truth.

This liberation from concentration on oneself is a new conversion, a *metanoia*, a real inner transformation. You begin to see that a true interior life is not your *own* life within the depths of your *own* being. It is the coming of the risen Christ into your being, from which you have previously *gone out*, in order to make room for Him. His presence gives you a true interior life, a basic purity of heart which will lead you to unity of spirit.

But the paradox of this inner liberation through humility can present a real ascetic problem. Can the deepest center of man truly be subjected to a spiritual method? Isn't it rather the heart, as the center of one's true self, which should subject all other levels of life to itself? Precisely how is the human spirit disciplined by humility? These are difficulties which are both doctrinal and practical, and their solution can greatly enhance the value of this central method of monastic spirituality.

Strictly speaking, the heart or spirit can be directly disciplined only by God. By man it is purified not directly, but only indirectly. This is because its function is to orient, integrate, and unify all other dimensions of man's being which it does by acting through powers of the soul and body distinct from itself. This integrating function is why the heart is called "the substance of the soul" by Saint John of the Cross.

It seems, then, that the heart's purification can be achieved in three different but complementary ways:

-By selecting and fostering those actions of the body or of the intellectual powers which best express man's inner orientation to the total following of Christ.

-By eliminating as much as possible any action whatsoever on the part of the body or the mind, thus allowing the inner emptiness of man's spirit to open itself to the Holy Spirit with greater energy and a more total freedom. This is the peaceful movement toward total listening which in the Greek tradition is called *hesychia*, and in the Latin, *quies*.

-By receiving in this state of obedient silence the action of the Holy Spirit, who alone can directly touch, purify, and transform man's deepest self into Him who is "life-giving Spirit" (I Cor. 15:45).

These three different ways of disciplining the heart explain the different elements of Benedictine humility. Obedience and silence correspond respectively to the first two indirect ways of cultivating the true self. They both involve bodily and mental control, though in differing proportions, and only for the sake of inner transformation. Emphasis is thus put on the inner, subjective grace of obedience, as we saw it in Chapter Five. Interior humiliation, on the other hand, as described in RB 7, 47-54 ("I am a worm and no man"), is a first result of this new "hidden man of the heart," as paradoxical as it may appear. It is a first fruit of direct purification. The Spirit is touching man's spirit. A new self is developing. True love is already present, soon to make itself manifest in the soul, the body, and the community.

Benedictine and even Cistercian spirituality tends not to analyze this process of direct purification as much as other spiritual movements, such as the Carmelite tradition, do. The monk's emphasis is on a simple, constant inner attitude of faith, and on exterior perseverance. Each human heart has a very personal path to follow in this regard, a path of beauty and of darkness. The sacrifice of self is consummated in the secret fire of inner tribulation, and this is not always easy to understand, either for the person involved or for those with whom he lives.

The reality of inner purification is a constant of Christian living. It teaches the secrets of the kingdom of God in a way which is otherwise unable to be achieved. Benedictine humility, when properly understood, has proven to be a reliable map along the way. Merely human motivations, which can often underlie zeal in observance or even the search for continual prayer, have to die. I myself must "be reduced to nothing, to a state of unknowing" (RB 7, 50), so that a new heart, that of Jesus Himself, takes the place of my former heart:

> All those works which formerly he had not fulfilled without fear, he will now begin to do by reason of this love, without any effort, as though naturally and by habit, no longer from the fear of hell, but rather from the love of Christ (RB 7, 68-69).

This analysis of Benedictine humility brings out very clearly its mystical quality. Old and young alike should pay attention to cenobitic obedience, silence, and humility not merely as corporal or mental exercises (which they necessarily are), but above all as disciplines of the spirit which are necessary for true fraternal charity and have a transforming effect throughout the human psyche. The spirit of monastic profession, especially of the vow of obedience, requires that we go beyond the letter of RB 5-7 to the true meaning of these chapters as indicated in the scriptural passages quoted there.

As in the case of the basic corporal disciplines, we can foresee a renewed appreciation of these more spiritual elements of monastic experience. They will be seen and lived not as factors of self-alienation, which they may appear to be to an unliberated heart, but as necessary purifying disciplines of one's true self, leading to self-transcendence, inner unity, and fraternal compenetration through the fruits of the Spirit. The monk learns by experience that "the Lord Jesus...sent the Holy Spirit upon all men that He might inspire them from within to love God with their whole heart and their whole soul, with all their mind and all their strength (cf. Mk. 12:30) and to love one another as Christ loved them" (LG 40).

Saint Benedict frequently refers to just such an influence of the heart on the soul, the mind, and the body (RB Prol., 49; 5, 16; 7, 8-9 and 69-70; 20, 2-4). We have already seen it in connection with *contemplatio*. The spirit, purified by humility, overflows with its joyfully obedient and silently transforming love. All the other levels of human existence receive the good news. The purified heart broadens the horizons of the human mind, profoundly influencing the unconscious dimensions of man's being. It transforms and gives joyful strength to soul, body, community, and environment, consecrating and unifying them in the truth.

Continual humility thus assumes more importance in the monk's life than continual observance or even than certain forms of continual prayer. It condenses within itself the meaning of monastic profession, governs all other elements in Benedictine spirituality, and is itself a continual prayer, because Jesus is "humble of heart" (Mt. 11:29).

Practical Consequences

What does this threefold spiritual way mean for us in our daily life?

In the first place, we should have *confidence in our vocation* as monks. Our community life may seem to be haphazard at times; but if we are faithful to the basic monastic observances, to prayer, and to an inner attitude of obedience, this spiritual way will produce its effects in us, opening us to the Word and teaching us to be docile to the Spirit. The Christian contemplative life is seldom improvised. Let us be grateful for the tradition of which we form a part, which goes back in time to the prophets of the Old Testament and finds its perfect model in the virginal humility of Mary. Each one of us has to live this vocation in his or her own special way in order to pass it on to others.

Secondly, the most important factor in Benedictine method is the *spiritual quality of the milieu in which we live*. This milieu is both exterior to us and interior, but let us put the accent where both the Gospel and monastic tradition put it—on the humility of Christ. Thus it would be a mistake to be overly anxious about external details. It would betray a lack of faith and more than likely would be a projection onto others, or onto the material elements of our life, of our own spiritual shortcomings. Everything is a gift from God. The very limitations of our community are part of the Benedictine-Cistercian spiritual way.

Thirdly, many centuries of experience indicate that, in practice, the key to the humility of Christ is *openness of spirit* or manifestation of conscience. We should take the initiative and make ourselves, our thoughts, our desires, and our experiences known to a spiritual guide, the novice master, or the abbot. Such openness—summed up somewhat imperfectly in Saint Benedict's fifth degree of humility (RB 7, 44-48)— usually takes a certain time and is seldom without some stress or strain, but its fruit is the joy of being known and loved as you are. Real purity of love or growth in prayer is very seldom achieved without it, at least in our monasteries.

Saint Benedict emphasizes two other consequences of his spiritual program which have important repercussions on the life of the vows— spiritual experience and discretion.

Benedict stresses the fact that, if used well, his spiritual art will lead the monk to a *deep spiritual experience* which surpasses all words (RB 4, 76), an interior liberation in the love of Christ (RB Prol. 49, and 7, 69), and a direct illumination by the Holy Spirit (RB 7, 70). Both Cassian, in his ninth and tenth *Conferences*, and the Cistercian Fathers in their *Sermons* and writings repeat this teaching on spiritual experience, fruit of the Spirit's action in a heart made true by humility.

As both a means and an integral part of spiritual experience, *"discretion, mother of all virtues"* (RB 64, 19) is another key factor in monastic life. Like manifestation of conscience, which it presupposes, monastic discretion is oriented to a discernment of spirits. It is a judgment, either discursive or intuitive, of the rational faculties, which seeks the action of God's Word and Spirit in a concrete situation. In this sense it can truly be considered as a form of prayer, an application of the mind to the Word of God, a reading of the signs of the time.

Cassian exhorts us to discretion in his Conf. 2, but his treatment is somewhat inadequate for present day needs, due to the stress he puts on exterior imitation rather than on a scrutiny of the internal movements of the human spirit. It is true that beginners, and novices especially, need to abandon their own judgment and submit their spirit to exterior control, but imitation is only a necessary first step in the journey toward deeper maturity.

The true meaning of this "mother of virtue" can be summed up in a phrase which Saint Ignatius of Loyola coined as the key to his entire work—*discreta caritas*, "discreet charity." This is in fact the "prudence and charity" (RB 64, 14) which Saint Benedict requires of the abbot, the "wisdom" which he looks for in the mature monk (RB 7, 61; 21, 4; 31, 1; 53, 22; 64, 2; 66, 1). Any act of charity, any spiritual method or expression of the vowed life, must continually pass through the judgment of discretion (*dia-krisis*), which proportions the instruments of spiritual growth to the end in view, according to the abilities, situation, and grace of the individual or community.

This critical judgment is especially important as we assume personal responsibility, either individually or as a group, for our day-to-day living of monastic spirituality within a plurality of possibilities. Without developing here the practice of discernment, it may be helpful to list a few of the more important criteria which can and should be used:

-in general, the fruit of the Spirit indicated by Saint Paul in Galatians 5:22: love, joy, peace, patience, kindness, generosity, trust, humility, mildness, and self-restraint. These are signs of Christian wisdom. What is to be avoided is the opposite of *tacite conscientia*

(RB 7, 35)—interior uneasiness or aggressiveness, an attitude of self-centeredness and impatience.

-an agreement with the monastic experience of past generations, both within the Benedictine-Cistercian tradition and in other contemplative traditions. There are certain ascetic and spiritual facts of life which are a common ground of personal growth and must be respected in any prudent discernment process. This is especially true in the realms of obedience and chastity.

-a consistency between practice and theory, avoiding obvious contradictions between these two levels, both for the persons involved and for the community as a whole. For instance, it would be a mistake to wish to become either a hermit or a spiritual director if I have never really experienced a life of prayer in community. This criterion has special importance in matters of poverty.

-a healthy respect for the opinions of visitors, even of seculars, in the line of RB 61, 4. What do informed and spiritually sensitive people look for in the monk?

-the maintenance of an open spirit of dialogue and communion with the brothers of the community and between different generations. This fruit of the Spirit means openness not only to them as persons, but also to the different currents of thought which they represent and express. The past opens to the present and the present to the past. In this climate, truth can take root and grow, opening us all to the future.

3. PROFESSION
"ACCORDING TO THE RULE OF SAINT BENEDICT"

A somewhat juridical aspect of Benedictine-Cistercian spirituality is its mention in the act of profession. Such an aspect should not surprise us if we understand the principles which we saw in Chapter One. Thus it would seem advisable that the statement by which the young monk expresses his monastic profession contain some concrete description of the content of the vows. This has traditionally been done by the phrase, "according to the Rule of Saint Benedict," added after the mention of stability, conversion of life, and obedience. But what exactly does this phrase commit me to? What does it mean to "keep the Rule"? What is implied in being faithful to the grace of the Benedictine or Cistercian vocation?

Primacy of Conversatio

In the first place, the phrase "according to the Rule of Saint Benedict," should be taken as applying to *all the promises* of profession, and especially to that of *conversatio*, rather than merely to that of obedience. Our analysis of the vow of conversion of life, in Chapter Two, and the more general synthesis in the preceding pages of the present chapter, have shown that *conversatio* governs all the other promises of profession, even that of obedience.

We have also seen that the Rule is in function of this life program and that the latter is, implicitly or explicitly, the monk's chosen way of spiritual growth. It is the threefold ascetic life style by which he hopes to open his soul to the Word of God and purify his heart in dependence on the Spirit of Christ. Strictly speaking, therefore, and provided the words are well understood, it would suffice to make profession of "conversion of life according to the Rule of Saint Benedict."

The Dilemma

However, a serious difficulty is caused by the fact that the Rule of Saint Benedict contains many details of cenobitic life which seem to have very secondary importance. Some of these details are clearly out-of-date and reflect the times in which the Rule was written, such as excommunications, whippings, child oblates, ceremonies for the reception of guests, the order of the psalmody, and the setup of the novitiate. Do these elements oblige us by force of our profession? If so, then we should abandon the Rule as a point of reference. If not, how can we say that we live according to it?

This dilemma has influenced monastic reform movements in the western Church for over a thousand years and continues to be a thorny issue. The first Cistercians, in particular, with their search for greater austerity and a more balanced spiritual program, waved the banner of "the purity of the Rule." They meant by this the integral observance of its prescriptions, against the additions and modifications which Cluniac monasticism had introduced in behalf of the Rule's "spirit," i.e., charity. Yet, in practice, the Cistercians themselves introduced several important elements which considerably modify the Rule: lay brothers, elimination of children within the community, a General Chapter and regular visitations controlling the local abbot and community. Within a short time the Cistercians had a detailed code of minor prescriptions as a supplement to the Rule. In fact, in one way or another, all attempts at living "according to the Rule" have involved the use of some sort of supplementary legislation such as a Book of Usages or Constitutions. For its part, the Holy See has always understood the phrase, "profession according to the Rule of Saint Benedict," to include, at least implicitly, "and according to the Constitutions."

Are we then to take this phrase to mean simply living "according to the *spirit* of the Rule"? This would put the emphasis on the spiritual values inculcated by Saint Benedict: charity, humility, reverence, liturgical praise, fraternal service, obedience without delay, and the like. This has been, in fact, the interpretation given by some monastic Congregations to the vows of obedience, stability, and conversion of life. Such an interpretation introduces a healthy element of criticism and historical judgment which is lacking in an overly rigid and literal interpretation. Nevertheless, if our analysis of monastic *conversatio* is at all correct, the spirit of the Rule consists not only in such spiritual values, important as they may be, but also in a concrete life style which has for its purpose the assimilation of these values by the monk and his growth in them.

The solution to this dilemma, therefore, consists in seeing that the Rule contains not only the two aspects of "letter" (detailed prescriptions) and "spirit" (spiritual values), but also a third, intermediary dimension—*basic spiritual methods*, fundamental structures, essential disciplines. The spirit, which is ultimately the action of the Holy Spirit in the monk's purified heart, is certainly the central and final purpose of the Rule. Nevertheless, the specific contribution of Benedictine spirituality is the establishment of a sociologically verifiable and coherent life program characterized by what we have called a "triple way": basic corporal observances, the mental discipline of *lectio divina*, and humility of heart. Other, more objective structures, such as the abbatial office, the novitiate, or the Liturgy of the Hours, spring from the need for these basic disciplines and are in function of them. Any given community or Congregation will have to express these fundamental principles according to the needs of time and place. The result will be the concrete customs of the local community.

Thus the RB is neither a closed legal code nor a merely exhortative document. It is more like a musical score which gives the inspired themes and basic harmonies upon which the orchestra can and should improvise under the direction of a Master. The Rule's frequent appeals to fidelity presuppose a normal dose of creativity, growth, and discernment according to the charism of each brother, community, Congregation, or Order.

To put this another way, Benedictine-Cistercian monasticism chooses from among the *values* contained in the Gospel some to which it will give special attention, according to its contemplative cenobitic charism. It expresses and fosters these values by means of a few fundamental *methods*, or disciplines, with their corresponding objective structures, which define the monk's profession as a particular way of Christian life. Each local community will further incarnate these values and these spiritual methods in more *detail*, according to the psychological and cultural conditions of its members, and according to the graces which they receive.

Now of these three levels contained in the Rule of Saint Benedict, the one most specifically Benedictine is the intermediary one of its fundamental methods or structures. The chief reason why the Rule was written was to establish authenticity and harmony among these fundamental means of cenobitic spirituality. This is also the essential charism of Saint Benedict. He refers to it with modesty as "a basic probity of behavior and the beginnings of monastic life" (RB 73, 1). His Rule achieved its purpose so well that it has survived intact throughout the centuries as the principal document mediating the monastic grace to the western Church.

The monk's probity of life, however, is not just good observance. It includes the inner thrust of his total conversion to Christ. A proper understanding of the Benedictine vocation, and of monastic life in general, will be based on this total search for inner transformation. The *totality* of the monk's openness to the grace of Christ, as embodied in the inner balance of his spiritual art, seems to explain the monastic charism better than an emphasis on more partial factors such as Christian solitude, community, or eschatology, important though these are. The totality of our conversion is the positive counterpart to what is sometimes called the monk's lack of a secondary purpose to his life.

Profession "according to the Rule" thus means committing ourselves to its fundamental principles or structures. Throughout this book we have described these principles in their relation to the different vows. In this present chapter we have seen their harmony as interacting spiritual methods at the roots of the Benedictine tree. Their purpose is to transmit a spiritual way and a spiritual experience, not just a constellation of spiritual values, but also a corporal, intellectual, and spiritual way to interiorize these values and so become, in a truly personal manner, Christ.

These basic disciplines are the link between spirituality and profession. Fidelity looks both to the values and to these methods, adapting or disregarding lesser elements mentioned in the Rule or elsewhere, in function of this, its vital meaning. Detailed observances change with time and place. Basic structures remain as signs and instruments of the Gospel values leading to man's transformation in Christ.

For Further Reflection

1. When you entered the monastic or religious life were you seeking a spiritual way? Have you found what you were looking for?

2. Which of the three general spiritual methods of Benedictine spirituality appeals to you most? In which do you feel most united to Christ?

3. Can the "spirit" of the Rule be separated from its "letter"? How would you sum up its spirit?

Bibliography

Bacht, H. "Antonius und Pachomius," in B. Steidle, ed. *Antonius Magnus Eremita.* Studia Anselmiana 38. Rome: Pont. Inst. S. Anselmi, 1956, pp. 71-82.

Bouyer, L. *Introduction to Spirituality*, pp. 144-156.

Dechanet, J. M. *William of St. Theirry: The Man and His Work*, CS 10, 1972, pp. 99-101.

Deseille, P. *Principes de spiritualite monastique*, esp. pp. 35-47.

de Vogue, A. *La Regle de Saint Benoit*, Vol. IV, pp. 119-226.

————. "Sub Regula vel Abbate: The Theological Significance of the Ancient Monastic Rules," in B. Pennington, ed. *Rule and Life* (see below), pp. 21-64.

Gilson, E. *The Mystical Theology of St. Bernard.* New York and London: Sheed and Ward, 1939, pp. 44-59 and 127-129.

Hausherr, I. *Noms du Christ, et voies d'oraison.* Rome: Pont. Inst. Orientalium Studiorum, 1960, pp. 162-167.

Hortelano, A. *Moral Responsable.* Salamanca: Sigueme, 1969, pp. 64-95.

Kelsey, M. *Encounter with God.* Minneapolis: Bethany Fellowship, 1972.

Leclercq, J. "Profession According to the Rule of St. Benedict," in B. Pennington, ed., *Rule and Life* (see below), pp. 117-150.

Martin, V. "Notes of a Sociologist on the Role of the Rule in Cistercian Life," in B. Pennington, ed. *Rule and Life* (see below), pp. 169-183.

Merton, T. *The New Man.* New York: Farrar, Straus, 1961, esp. pp. 71-78.

————. *Zen and the Birds of Appetite.* New York: New Directions, 1968.

Miura, I. and Sasaki, R. F. *The Zen Koan.* New York: Harcourt, Brace, 1965, esp. pp. 35-46.

Moustakas, C., ed. *The Self: Explorations in Personal Growth.* New York: Harper and Row, 1956.

Nee, W. *The Release of the Spirit.* Indianapolis: Sure Foundation, 1965.

Pennington, B., ed. *Rule and Life*, CS 12, 1971, esp. pp. 1-20 and 208-212.

Salmon, P. "L'ascese monastique et les origines de Citeaux," in *Melanges Saint Bernard.* Dijon: Burgundian Association of Scholarly Societies, 1954, pp. 268-283. English translation in *Monastic Studies 3*. Pine City, New York: Mt. Saviour, 1965, pp. 123 ff.

Suzuki, D. T. *The Training of the Zen Buddhist Monk.* New York: University Books, 1965.

Vandenbrouke, F. *Why Monks?* pp. 23-91.

William of St. Thierry, *The Golden Epistle*, nn. 41-45.

CHAPTER EIGHT

CHALLENGE OF THE VOWS

We have been studying the vows individually and, in the last chapter, have seen them within their larger context of the methods of spirituality which characterize the monastic way of life. But there still remains the hard fact of daily existence. It is only here, in the reality of the present moment, that we meet Christ in a mutual commitment of love. It is only here that personal fulfillment can take place through a true gift of self and the Heart of God can transform the human heart. Preparation for profession ends here, and fidelity begins.

In other words, monastic profession, which springs from a living dialogue with Christ, is meant to lead the monk to an even more total dialogue with his Lord and Master. It is an *exchange of loves*, which the monk must first experience in order to make it the central melody of his personal harmony of grace and nature. Moreover, this dialogue has *universal repercussions*, since it takes place in the Body of Christ and in the name of all men. What follows is a final, more specific reference to the day-to-day flow of this inner life of the vows.

1. A LIFE OF LOVE

Commitment

We saw in the chapter on stability that a commitment in true love bridges the gap between person and community. The vows challenge us to walk this bridge and to grow in sensitivity to its demands. We can do so only if we build our life on the rock which is Christ, not on the sands of passing feelings, superficial motivations, or spiritual fads.

There is a double movement in this commitment which requires both generosity and flexibility. On the one hand, the outer forms of everyday life in community, which embody for each one of us the essential structures of the monastic vocation, are at the service of the monk's own uniqueness before God. On the other hand, however, this spiritual identity is only found in an act of total self-donation to one's particular community. This is because the monk is a lover of Christ, he finds his deepest existence in his relation to Christ, and Christ lives for him in this particular community with its particular history, make-up, problems, and graces.

The reality of Christ living in the local community helps us to appreciate the need for a definitive, life-long commitment as an essential element of monastic profession. A temporary experience of living in a monastic environment is both legitimate and very helpful for certain people, but it should not be taken as expressing a genuine monastic vocation. Nor does it represent the real center of spiritual gravity for the person involved, since this is, by its very name and nature, permanent, totally integrating and, in a way, eternal. The challenge of the vows consists, above all, in the totality of the gift of self to Christ living in one's particular local community. This may seem to an outsider to be an unwarranted limitation of the Gospel, but, for him who receives the call, it is its concrete application and logical consequence.

Actually, man's unique personhood in Christ is never independent of his immediate environment, nor of the basic values which mold and govern the milieu in which he lives. The unity and interplay of these different forces at work around us are what give shape and meaning to human existence.

For a monk, the "wedding" of the various levels of his vocational commitment—personal uniqueness, community environment, Christian and monastic values—into an harmonious consonance in daily life is the central concern of his formation. In fact the period of initiation can be understood as the time to discern whether such a "wedding" is conducive to the deepest unfolding of the young monk's life in Christ and to the good of the community he wants to join.

In this process of assimilation, discernment, and inner growth, monastic profession represents a moment of clarification and unity. Objectively, the way ahead is understood, at least in its essential contours. Subjectively, experience has taught us our capacities and our limitations. The judgment of discernment has been made and our commitment to Christ is stronger and more lucid than when we entered the monastery. The different vows are, more than anything else, key factors in clarifying this commitment. They are meant to make it more realistic, "in order to derive more abundant fruit from this baptismal grace" (LG 44). They are meant to put this baptismal commitment in greater contact with daily life and its mixture of joys and sorrows, spiritual values and humble obligations, interiority, and service. The vows assume your daily life and center it on Christ.

Diagram III attempts to sum up the meaning of the vows by means of an image which shows not only their external obligations, but also their unity as distinct expressions of one spiritual dynamism and their intrinsic relation to the Person of Christ.

Diagram III

THE MEANING OF MONASTIC PROFESSION:
A PILGRIMAGE IN RESPONSE TO A CALL

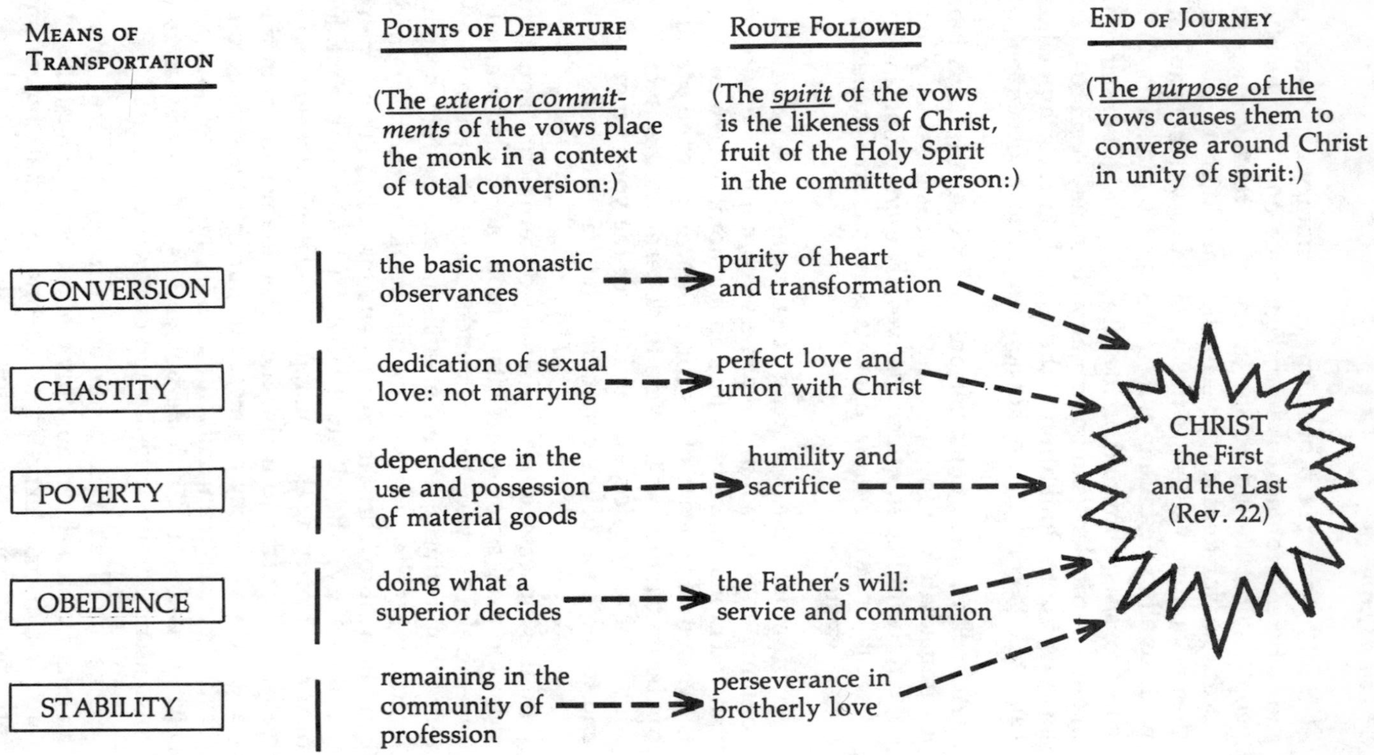

MEANS OF TRANSPORTATION	POINTS OF DEPARTURE	ROUTE FOLLOWED	END OF JOURNEY
	(The _exterior commitments_ of the vows place the monk in a context of total conversion:)	(The _spirit_ of the vows is the likeness of Christ, fruit of the Holy Spirit in the committed person:)	(The _purpose_ of the vows causes them to converge around Christ in unity of spirit:)
CONVERSION	the basic monastic observances	purity of heart and transformation	
CHASTITY	dedication of sexual love: not marrying	perfect love and union with Christ	CHRIST the First and the Last (Rev. 22)
POVERTY	dependence in the use and possession of material goods	humility and sacrifice	
OBEDIENCE	doing what a superior decides	the Father's will: service and communion	
STABILITY	remaining in the community of profession	perseverance in brotherly love	

Gift

To have been called to make these vows and to live them is a very great grace, a special gift from God. The life which they open up to us enables us to follow Christ more perfectly in the simplicity of the Gospel counsels, as a gift of our love in return for His. Jesus constantly repeats to each one of us what he told the woman at the well: "If you knew the gift of God and who he is that asks you for a drink, you yourself would have asked him, and he would have made you the gift of living water" (Jn. 4:10).

If we give our love to Jesus day by day in the humble path of the Gospel, it is because we have seen in faith that He Himself is the great love-gift of the Father to us. Jesus, in turn, bestows on us "the gift of living water," the Holy Spirit. Our fidelity to Christ is based on His own fidelity—and the Father's—to us.

The vows are made and lived within this overwhelming reality of the divine Self-Gift. It is the *paschal mystery*. The liturgy initiates us into it. God not only calls us, but also gives us the means to respond to His call. These means are above all the Eucharist, the other sacraments, and all the rest of the Church's life which revolves around them. The life of the vows, like all personal effort, must be a preparation for, or a consequence of, the monk's participation in God's plan for his eternal fulfillment in Christ.

When Jesus asks us to give everything over to Him and follow Him in His paschal mystery, He is inviting us to death and to new life. He invites us to the love which He has for us and to the knowledge of the Father, "whom no one knows but the Son, and anyone to whom the Son wishes to reveal Him" (Mt. 11:27). He wishes us to learn about Himself and the Father through the Gospels, through prayer, the sacraments, and our brothers. But above all He asks us to imitate Him and share His life in body, soul, and spirit. This will inevitably involve suffering, the cross.

Without the cross of Christ in our life we are not responding adequately to God's Self-Gift:

> The third step of humility is that a person for love of God submit himself to his superior in all obedience, imitating the Lord, of whom the Apostle says, "He became obedient even unto death"...And to show how those who are faithful ought to endure all things, however contrary, for the Lord, the Scripture says in the person of those who are suffering, "For your sake we are put to death all the day long; we are considered as sheep marked for slaughter." Then, sure in their hope of a divine recompense, they go on with joy to declare, "But in all these trials we overcome, through Him who has given us His love" (RB 7, 34-39).

If at times it is exasperating to "share by patience in the sufferings of Christ and thus deserve to have a share also in His kingdom" (RB Prol., 50), we should look at Mary, who followed Jesus in His passion, letting herself be wounded for the glory of God and the salvation of men. Her example and intercession will give us strength to sacrifice a human, insignificant joy in order to give ourselves more fully to God and to our brothers.

A life based on the cross of Christ will have a deep joy all its own, which is not to say that it will be easy. Real happiness springs from love. True love means the gift of oneself and, consequently, sacrifice. Jesus told this to us shortly before consummating His own self-offering: "I have fulfilled the commandments of my Father and abide in His love. I have told you this so that my joy may be yours and your joy may be complete" (Jn. 15:10-11).

At the very moment in which He initiated His passion, He gave us His joy, which consists in fulfilling the will of His Father in all things. This is also the source of the monk's joy. Sooner or later we are going to find ourselves nailed to the cross by our vows. This is not just a pious phrase but an inner necessity of true life. It will be precisely the cross which we would prefer not to carry. Jesus, however, calls "Happy the poor in spirit, because their is"—here and now—"the kingdom of heaven" (Mt. 5:3). The lives of the saints confirm the paradox:

> One of the holy Fathers said to the monks who asked him about the reason for renunciation: My sons, it is right that we should hate all rest in this present life, and hate also pleasures of the body and the joys of the belly. Let us not seek honor from men. Then our Lord Jesus Christ will give us heavenly honors, rest in eternal life, and glorious joy with His angels.

Even now, a life of self-emptying for love of Jesus Christ will not be sad, confused, or bitter. If we have left all things, even good things, it is in order to rise to a new life here and now, in spirit, mind, and body. It is to love better and to show more clearly to all men the love of the Father, which Jesus has given us. We must learn to let ourselves be invaded more fully by this love, in order to let the Beloved live His own life more completely in us.

How can we live out such a commitment of total love? The necessary graces are obtained only by constant and humble prayer. So we have an obligation to pray. Is it not the absence of prayer, of serious reading, and of solid convictions concerning the realities of faith, which gives to certain monks and nuns that lack of grace, that religious tepidity which at times is painfully evident? This is despite the fact that they are otherwise friendly persons and relatively faithful in their duties. Such a lack of inner spiritual strength shows the need for going beyond profession.

BEYOND PROFESSION

Our prayer and God's gift of the Spirit are not merely for the sake of external behavior, or even for interior enthusiasm. The divine initiative becomes indispensable from the fact that monastic life is only truly nourished by constant spiritual contact with the glorified Humanity of Christ the Savior, who lives in us by His Spirit. Jesus thus becomes the principle of a new life: "The life which I live is not my own; Christ is living in me" (Gal. 2:20). We have seen this especially in regard to Christian chastity, and as the final meaning of the vow of conversion, but it applies to every aspect of our life. The foundation of all existence is the life of the risen Christ (cf. Col. 1:16-18). The life of a monk is immersed in the depths of this new life, which is both Christ's life in the Church and the Church's life in Christ. The monk becomes essentially a man of the Church.

This insertion into the living Christ explains in what sense monastic profession, and religious profession in general, is a consecration of our entire existence to God (LG 44 and PC 5). We have referred to this reality in almost all previous chapters but now we can understand it more fully. Jesus, the Incarnate Word of God, was christened by His own divine Sonship from the time of His conception in Mary's womb. This divine anointing—the hypostatic union—became visibly messianic throughout His public life, especially at certain key moments such as His baptism and temptation, the choice and instruction of the apostles, His transfiguration and miracles, the Passion and, above all, at His resurrection from the dead (Acts 2:36). The consecrated Humanity of Christ, in turn, sanctifies all creation by His messianic activity (AG 5). This whole process is the "consecration in truth" to which Jesus refers in John 17:17-19.

Such an ontological contact and living incorporation into the Messias (the Christ, the Anointed One), who is the Only Son of God, is the reality underlying the different terms: *sanctified, consecrated, anointed, Christian!* In faith and baptism each Christian receives this consecration in a manner similar to that in which the Humanity of Christ received His Divinity. The grace of the risen Christ becomes ours. His life must express itself at all levels of our life. It will come to the surface with special force, however, at certain key moments when, by docility to the Holy Spirit, our Christian activity is channeled toward specific forms of the Church's—that is, of the risen Christ's—mission. These are often moments of fundamental option when we are "consecrated in truth."

Religious or monastic profession is one of these key events. It is a specification of the baptismal consecration according to the shared grace and mission of each Order or Congregation. The Spirit of Christ, working in the Church and through the abiding grace of baptism, consecrates the gift of self which He Himself inspired. The consecratory prayers of the profession rite point beyond themselves to this inner consecration.

True religious life is thus the life of the Spirit of Christ in His Church. It is the life that flows from contact with Christ crucified who has become, through resurrection, "life-giving spirit" (I Cor. 15:45). The spirit of the vows is, then, to think and love and act not just as Christ *would* act in a given situation, but as He precisely *does* act, by His Spirit and grace in us at the moment. It is to live and act with the mind of the Church, which is the mind of Christ.

In other words, monastic profession is something more than imitation from afar, a moral reproduction in our lives of a pattern offered by Jesus in the Gospels. We do not simply open the Gospels, the Rule, the monastic Fathers, or books such as the present one, and then by our own power, ingenuity, and good will put into effect, humanly, the things which we read. Such efforts are necessary, but unless they are on a deeper plane they have little fruit for our spirit. A well-known episode from the desert experience illustrates this deeper need:

> Abba Lot came to Abba Joseph and said: Father, according as I am able, I keep my little rule, and my little fast, my prayer, meditation and contemplative silence; and according as I am able I strive to cleanse my heart of thoughts: now what more should I do? The elder rose up in reply and stretched out his hands to heaven, and his fingers became like ten lamps of fire. He said: Why not be totally changed into fire?

The life of the vows, then, must go beyond the vows themselves and beyond the spiritual methods which we use. It must go to Christ Himself who dwells in us by the grace of faith and inspires our thoughts and acts by the inner flame of His Spirit. He will reveal a new life, within your deepest self and yet infinitely beyond it, a life of love and inner transformation in which the different Gospel counsels find their true meaning.

So let us never forget that the action of the Holy Spirit in our lives is vitally necessary. The monk who forgets his insertion into Christ and his continual dependence on "the gift of living water" will slowly but surely work himself into a position where he will be unfaithful in small things or great. Yet his very infidelities will be permitted by God to awaken him to new compunction, to the realization of his need for the Spirit, perhaps to a new understanding of Mary's spiritual maternity over him, and of Christ's loving compassion for him in his weakness.

Let us always pray for the grace to keep our eyes open, to live in vigilance, lest we lose the delicacy of conscience that we need to respond day after day to the Lord who calls us to Himself and gives us a special mission among His people. He has become incarnate for us in a specific way of life and in a specific community so that we can fulfill this mission. Let us not claim to walk in the Spirit, to love our brothers, and to love prayer if in fact our attitude is one of carelessness toward our vows, for they, too, are gifts of His love.

2. IN THE NAME OF ALL MEN

The mission of the Christian monk at the present crossroads of human history is too important to warrant taking lightly the obligations of profession. No one else can achieve, to the degree that he can and in the name of all men, mankind's true vocation. It is worth reflecting on two final texts which illustrate this great reality of the monk's role in world history:

> The Christian is certainly bound by need and by duty to struggle with evil through many afflictions and to suffer death; but, as one who has been made a partner in the paschal mystery, and as one who has been configured to the death of Christ, he will go forward, strengthened by hope, to the resurrection.
>
> All this holds true not for Christians only but also for all men of good will in whose hearts grace is active invisibly. For since Christ died for all, and since all men are in fact called to one and the same destiny, which is divine, we must hold that the Holy Spirit offers to all the possibility of being made partners, in a way known to God, in the paschal mystery. Such is the nature and the greatness of the mystery of man as enlightened for the faithful by the Christian revelation. Christ has risen again, destroying death by His death, and has given life abundantly to us so that, becoming sons in the Son, we may cry out in the Spirit, "Abba, Father!" (GS 22).

> In present-day society, which so easily rejects God and denies His existence, the life of men and women completely dedicated to the contemplation of eternal truth constitutes an open profession of the reality of both His existence and His presence, since such a life seeks that loving intimacy with God which "bears witness to our spirit that we are sons of God" (Rom. 8:16). Hence, whoever leads such a life can efficaciously reassure both those who suffer temptations against faith and those who through error are led to be skeptical about the possibility man might have of conversing with the transcendent God (VS 5).

The call to live the monastic vows is a call to guide the human family toward its true destiny, which is divine, its paschal passover to the place of communion for those who seek God today. Above all, however, he fulfills his vocation by touching the hearts of men through the Heart of Christ. Saint Seraphim of Sarov said it to his fellow Russians of the nineteenth century, having learned it himself in silence and solitude: "Have peace in your heart and thousands around you will be saved."

This is what it means for the monk to live his personal consecration in the truth: through the humble process of monastic life, through perseverance in faith, docility, praise, and fraternal love, the power of God is released into the world of today. The monk finds that through his experience of Christ he has become a father of the world to come, a prince of peace, the first fruits of a new humanity.

The purpose of each vow, and of all the vows taken as a whole, is to aid this divine work, in which personal poverty is made perfect in the depths of the soul, conversion is a transformation in the silence of love, chastity becomes virginity of intellect and spirit, stability roots us in the kingdom of Christ, and obedience grows into dependence on the Holy Spirit in every moment of our life. Let us glory, then, in our poverty and weakness, for with the help of Mary, Mother of Christ, our profession will carry us, weak as we are, deep into the mystery of the Cross and Resurrection of the Lord Jesus.

For Further Reflection

1. Are the exterior commitments of profession clear in your mind? Which of the vows do you think is the most important for you? Which will unite you most with Christ?

2. How would you describe your relation to Jesus at this moment of your life? Does this correspond to your deepest personal identity?

3. How do you personally experience your insertion into the Church? Are you satisfied with the way in which you are fulfilling your mission in regard to all men, your brothers? How can you deepen this mission?

Bibliography

Coleman, P. "Psychological Aspects of Commitment by Monastic Vow," in Region of the Isles, *Symposium on the Vows*, pp. F1-F14.

de H. Doherty, C. *The Gospel Without Compromise*. Notre Dame: Ave Maria Press, 1976.

Kelly, C. "Monastic Commitment as a Human Phenomenon," in Region of the Isles, *Symposium on the Vows*, pp. 1-25.

Merton, T. *A Thomas Merton Reader*. New York: Harcourt, Brace, 1962, pp. 337-365.

Rees, D., et al. *Consider Your Call*, pp. 128-136.

Van Kaam, A. *In Search of Spiritual Identity*. Denville, New Jersey: Dimension Books 1975.

_____.*On Being Involved*. Denville, New Jersey: Dimension Books, 1970.

INDEX

Abbot, 5, 14, 21, 84, 99; Benedictine poverty and, 67-70, 75-77; duties, 23-24, 28, 69-70, 146; representing Christ, 70, 72, 81, 90, 115, 145. *See also* Superior

Ad Gentes, 16, 28, 85, 103, 157

Aelred of Rievaulx, St., 58

Agape, 53-55, 62-63, 114-115. *See also* Charity, Love

Anthony of the Desert, St., 11, 18, 107-108, 125-126

Anthropology, 130-134; of Cistercians, 130-132; of St. Benedict, 130, 132, 133; of Thomas Merton, 132; patristic, 130-131

Aquinas, Thomas, St., 66-67, 105, 133

Art, spiritual, 42, 127-129, 135, 146, 150

Asceticism, 10-40, 123-129; basic principle, 111-112, 139; prayer and, 10-13, 42, 62-63, 120. *See also* Austerity, Conversion of life, Monasticism

Austerity, 25-27; chastity and, 53-57

Baptism, chastity and, 50, 53; conversion of life and, 33, 37, 38, 41, 129; grace of, 153, 157-159, *see also* Grace; obedience and, 81, 86-87; poverty and, 77; spiritual methods and, 129; stability and, 115

Basil, St., 27, 78

Benedict, St., degrees of humility, 40, 57, 128, 130-131, 144-146, 155; development of monastic life and, 5-8, 13-14, 124-129; essential charism, 150; on chastity, 46-47; on conversion, 13-14; on discre-tion, 146; on obedience, 83-87, 91-95; on poverty, 67-70; on prayer, 21, 24, 25, 26; on purity of heart, 39-40, 131-132, 144-145; on stability, 98-100, 112-116; on wisdom, 146; on work, 29-32; Rule of, *see* Rule; three dimensions of man, 130-131, 132-134, 144-145

Benedictine-Cistercian, anthropological roots, 130-135; balance, 137-139, 150; basic structures, 133-134, 136-137, 149-150; core of, 140-141, 145; historical roots of spirituality, 10-13, 123-129; life, 42, 135; observances, *see* Monastic observances; poverty, 66-79; profession and, 123-124, 147-148, 150; spirituality, 56-57, 123-150; stability, 98-121; theological roots, 129, 134-137; vows, 10, 154

Bernard, St., common will, 131; conversion of life, 14, 83-89; humility, 142; on free will, 131; stability, 108-109; Virgin Mary, 136

Bruno, St., 18

Cassian, John, 11, 12-13, 31, 99; monastic renunciations, 12-13; on conversion of life, 12-13, 126; purity of heart, *see* Purity of heart; three dimensions of man, 130; unity of love, 21, 130

Celibacy, 49-50. *See also* Chastity

Charity, as spirit of RB, 13, 148; contemplative, 7, 32, 38, 116; discretion and, 147; evangelical

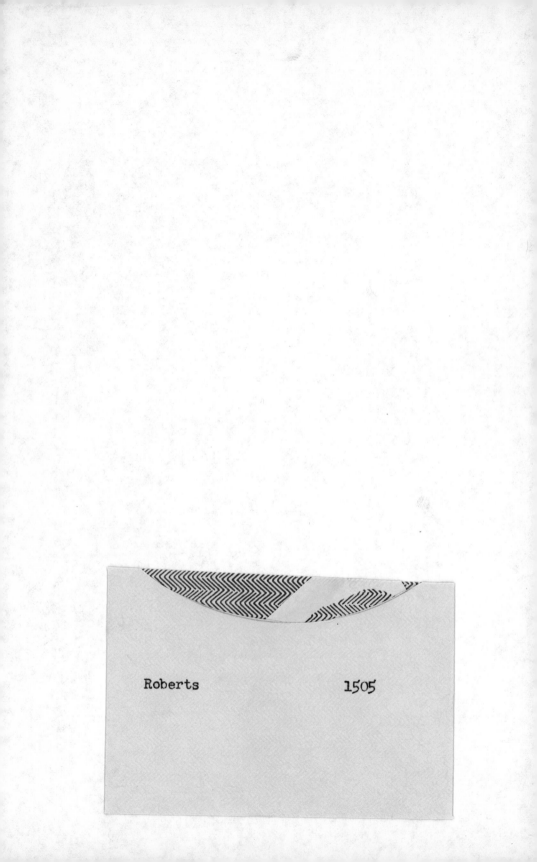

Roberts   1505